the exerciser

Sol Weinstein &
Howard Albrecht

the exerciser

Combustoica
a prose project of About Comics - Camarillo, California

In Memoriam

BOBBY DARIN

SAM RABINOWITZ

JACKIE KANNON
Of the Ratfink Room.

The characters in this book are wholly fictional. Any resemblance, by name or otherwise, to persons living or dead is purely coincidental, accidental, or typographical.

Copyright © 1974 by Sol Weinstein and Howard Albrecht. All rights reserved.
Ballantine Books edition: April, 1974
Combustoica edition: April, 2014

Published by Combustoica, a prose project of About Comics
WWW.COMBUSTOICA.COM

Dedications

Ellie, David and Judy Weinstein;
Bernice, Shellee and Richard Albrecht
Sam and Chai Soora Weinstein;
Ada Albrecht;
Harry and Bess Eisner; Stan Eisner;
Ronn Owens;
Dr. and Mrs. Howard S. Friedman;
and James J. Shapiro

With Special Thanks To:
Dr. Elliot A. Harris and Dr. Donald W. Luber
For their technical assistance and Valium.

Thence He spent forty days and forty nights in the wilderness fasting and being tempted by the devil. And the devil spake unto Him saying, "Wouldst thou lift up thy hand to smite me and gainsay my presence upon this earth?" Whereupon He answered, "Later. First I've got to grab a little lunch."

St. Matthew 14:3
St. John 13:7
(in overtime)

It is easier for a camel to ascend into heaven through the eye of a needle than to get a three-room, $110-a-month apartment (rent-controlled)...

Mrs. Maria Rodriguez,
welfare client 678890

If I am not alone, then does it not follow that I am with someone?

Pope Sol
(The Pretender)

prologue

The House

     The house. The house of Colin and Camille Carew at 54 Dovedroppings Lane. It sat twenty feet from the litter-free roadway, nestled smugly on its billiard table of a manicured lawn, on whose verdure no patches of crabgrass or periwinkle would have dared to attempt an insidious beachhead, so savagely protective was Bandini (not the ten-pound bag of commercial weed-killer, but Salvatore Bandini, the Carew's eagle-eyed gardener, who had destroyed more suspicious growths than chemotherapy treatments at Mount Sinai Hospital).
  The house. It preened. Gloated. Was bitchily pleased with what it was and what it symbolically stood for. If its 3300 square feet of rafters, radiant heating coils, plasterboard walls, and roof shingles could magically have come to life and verbalized its conceit, its hubris, it would have bellowed this defiant shout to the world: "I am a Levittown Country Clubber, the crème de la crème of Lower Bucks County, Pennsylvania, who has shot up in value in less than a quarter-century from seventeen-nine-oh-oh to forty-five G's, thanks to faultless engineering, esthetic loveliness, and a perfectly marvelous crime rate which is chasing middle-class America out of the inner cities.
  "Look at my fabulous appointments and lick your lips... my galvanized drainpipes and gutters flashing in the sun... my rows of azaleas, so swollen with 86-proof nectar that the honeybees swigging from their stamens and pistils, as inebriated as corporate executives after a six-martini

lunch, can not even summon the strength to fly back to their hives, but must wait to get a lift home on the brawny back of some passing Junebug (a praying mantis, if they're religious fanatics)... and my elfin lawn jockey, which my owners judiciously repainted white. *We shall overcome.*

"Ah, all praises be to you, oh William J. Levitt, you, the Christopher Wren of the rec room, the Frank Lloyd Wright of the carport... had Henrik Ibsen lived to have known you, surely he would have called *you* The Master Builder... you who possessed the vision, the dream, and FHA financing to bulldoze the farmlands where once the immortal William Penn sat under a great oak, writing to his Penn pals, so that I and all my fellow Country Clubbers could be given life in a few frantic hours of men rushing about with saws, hammers, toilets under their sinewy arms, pouring concrete, nailing two-by-fours, all of which led a sage to note that although Rome wasn't built in a day, Levittown was."

The house at 54 Dovedroppings Lane. It and the others of its august class, Country Clubbers on Larkleavings Lane and Drakedreck Road and Swallowspoor Boulevard, dominated the landscape, dwarfed only by Levittown's lone skyscraper, the awe-inspiring golden arches of a McDonald's, reaching nearly thirty feet into the blue, cloudless horizon.

On a soft breeze came the customary sounds of suburban life. The bursting jackets of Oscar Mayer wieners on a thousand glowing backyard barbecues, which brought to mind sustained artillery barrages in the Sinai. The smooth, even humming of the power mowers, equalled only by similar humming on controversial White House tapes. The soft, piteous whimpering of a Little League shortstop upon learning that he had been traded, not to another team, but to another family, because (in his father's choked voice), "I love you, Sheldon, but you're just not hitting."

Yes, the house on 54 Dovedroppings Lane. Quiet, homey, carefree. And yet it was this very structure that was destined for an ordeal of horror that would rock it to the very roots of its willow trees. How odd that such a sanctuary of serenity would be gripped by the icy tentacles of a force beyond credulity. But why here? Traditionally horror found its natural habitat in the mist-shrouded ambience of the wild Carpathian mountains: a young couple motoring through an ebon night, finding their Essex touring car sputtering, then conking out; a violent storm that sends ugly, jagged lightning flashing against the turrets of a castle; the young people thunderously banging a knocker shaped like a bat's head against an oaken door, the door creaking open, a bloodless face peeking out of a black cape, its vile, vaselined lips twisted into a sinister smile... "Good evening. I perceive your car has broken down, and to make things even groovier the bridge has been washed away by the storm. Ain't that a kick in the coffin? Perhaps you will do me the honor of spending the night in my castle. Igor, show the gentleman to his vault, and you, his lovely wife, may I say that's a hell of a throat you got there, sweetie..." Or in a tiny Germanic hamlet usually called Goldstadt where villagers in lederhosen stop dancing on grapes and singing the Song of the New Wine long enough to gather up torches and chase a lumbering, mindless, fifteen-foot-tall being through the gnarled limbs of a tortured forest, while the creature's creator, a mild-mannered, bespectacled young man in a white laboratory jacket, shrugs and says, "Monster? Who knows from monsters? According to all my calculations, I was supposed to be making a ten-speed bike..." Or by the flickering fire in a small gypsy encampment where a hulking, disheveled English lord opens his tormented heart to a Romany crone. "Maria, I am cursed. Look, look in my hand, the sign of the Pentagon." "Lawrence, my son, you mean Pentagram." "No, Maria, Pentagon. I was bitten by a werehawk. Soon the moon will be full and I must kill again. Can't you hide me?" "Lawrence, get in the back of the wagon and I will lock you in until the spell passes. Remember, 'even a man who is pure at heart and says his prayers by night/can become a werewolf when the wolfbane blooms so bright.' That's not exactly a Hal David lyric, but what do you want from an old Romany crone? Here, eat a can Campbell's Cream of

Wolfbane Soup, the Manhandler, go inside and suck on a silver bullet, and I'll let you out in three days. Four the most..." Or in a creepy old apartment house on Central Park inhabited by a coven of witches and warlocks where a flat-chested girl promises she will bear Satan's child if he will grant her a magnificent set of mammae, the chilling tale known throughout the literature of the diabolic as *Rosemary's Boobies.*

This was horror in all its classicism, in these hideous locales from which it drew its Satanic nourishment—Transylvania, Goldstadt, Romany, the Bramford. But Levittown? *Levittown?* The most horrible events in this bastion of the good life occurred when the Safeway supermarket decided to drop S & H Green Stamps, or the Seven-Eleven store ran out of Tuborg Beer, the beer with class, or you found out, all TV commercials to the contrary, that your highly reputed Maytag washer actually needed a service call.

But genuine, bloodcurdling, spine-tingling, hair-raising horror was indeed headed on a collision course with this sylvan suburban outpost. The four great winds of the world, which know all that transpires below in the domiciles of men, had picked up sinister vibrations from a mysterious place and now were passing along the evil tidings. The North Wind passed them to the West Wind, the West Wind to the South Wind, the South to the East, the East to Dollar Bill Bradley, who passed to Walt Frazier who passed to Willis Reed who slam dunked two points, until the chain of passage connected up with its last link, a gentle breeze in Levittown which until that moment had done nothing more malicious than lift up the skirt of a student at the Bucks County Library. Suddenly that breeze, now itself a harbinger of evil, began an inexplicable whipping of the area, scooping up copies of the *Times-Courier* on 17,000 porches and spinning them end over end like tumbleweeds. The area's fauna, like animals all over the globe whose sixth senses pick up impending catastrophes such as earthquakes and monsoons long before humans do, began to act in an irrational manner.

Dogs bayed mournful howls, crept into their $49.50 Sears prefab doghouses, thrusting their tails between their legs. On Ptarmiganturd Lane a pure-bred boxer, whose tail had been clipped humiliatingly, did the best he could and thrust his legs between his legs. A finicky fat cat named Morris did the unthinkable, pushed away a bowl heaped high with 9-Lives tuna, and clambered up a maple tree in his anxiety. Even nature's tiniest denizens manifested the terror they knew was at hand. The aforementioned Junebug sent a message from its antennae that it would not show up until the following January. Glowworms and lightning bugs went into self-imposed brownouts so that whatever horror was coming would not notice them. Even ants deserted their ant farms (thereby forfeiting generous Department of Agriculture subsidies) to burrow deeper into the loam, praying they too would be spared.

On went the ceaseless murmur of the wind... *It's coming, it's coming, it's coming...*

And Levittown, that divine green oasis of felicity, would never be the same.

I: The Beginning

All the world's a stage, so let's rob it.

JESSE JAMES

one

"Gentlemen," Levi Flare, the brilliant young television director, spoke into his intercom to the cameramen deployed around the floor of Studio Two in the Liberty Bell Productions complex on Philadelphia's City Line Avenue. "Pictures, please."

The young men, casually attired in the blue denim jackets and jeans which made so many millions of Americans look as though they'd just done a stretch in Attica, stubbed out their smokes and took their positions. The stage lights went up and an audience of some three hundred women of varying shapes and sizes began to squeal. Having completed their chores, the stagehands leaned back on packing crates to watch Colin Carew prepare to do his devastating thing again. A stage manager opened his striped clapboard to Camera One to slate the take, said, "Five, four, three, two, one," cued Colin in the wings with an index finger, a red camera eye winked on, screaming broke out when the applause sign flashed on, and Carew, a six-foot, lanky young man dressed in a fashionable Pierre Cardin safari suit, gave his dry-look shag haircut a final pat and bounced onto centerstage to the swinging uptempo of a ten-piece jazz band.

For fully fifteen seconds, the women, who had waited for months for the prized tickets to the taping and then hours outside for favored seating, set up a din that smothered his attempts to launch into an opening monologue until he finally stilled it with a pleading hand gesture.

"Jolly good to see you, my luvs," he chirped in his impeccable Oxonian accent. "Like my safari suit?"

"Yes, yes," several ladies screamed. "It's darling, Colin, darling..."

"Well—now get this—safari, so goody." And his sparkling, prewritten ad lib sent a round of titters through the horde. "I wore this suit the last time I was gathering recipes from the Masai in East Africa. And I love Africa. While I was there I saw a baby elephant... too small to have a trunk, but he did have an overnight bag." He giggled.

Uproarious laughter.

"Please, lady," and he bent over to a first-row occupant whose eyes were cascading tears of jollity, "if you're going to laugh that hard keep your legs crossed. The seats in here aren't Sanforized!" He giggled again.

Another detonation of hilarity.

"But I love Africa with its strange flora and fauna. You know Flora and Fauna, that's a dance team at the Holiday Inn in Kenya. And Tarzan swinging home to the treehouse on the 5:45 vine. Of course, they have vines in Israel, too. There they call 'em—now get this—Manischewitz vines." He giggled a third time.

Pandemonium.

"Oh, Colin," and he kissed the tips of his fingers, "you're hot tonight."

On cue, ever eager to perpetuate a running gag, bandleader Barney Baines broke in to call out. "How... hot... are... you?"

The ladies leaned forward, anticipating another sparkling ad lib from their hero.

Colin did not disappoint them. "I'm so hot, so hot, that my jockey shorts are getting mash notes from Secretariat. But that's what I get for horsing around."

Pandemonium plus.

"Well, luvs, it's work time." Carew snapped a finger, a fanfare blasted out of the trumpet section, and the curtain parted to reveal a set designed as an ultramodern kitchen with stainless steel counters, a two-door Amana freezer, shiny copper pots and kettles dangling from hooks, ladles, knives, and spatulas laid out as though they were surgical instruments, plus rack upon rack of seasonings, a host of mixing bowls, a microwave oven, and all the other accouterments of this *Good Housekeeping Magazine* dream come true.

A skillet in hand, he said, "Today, my luvs, we're going to take a jolly old leaf out of my good friend Monty Hall's book and call the first half of our show—now get this—Let's Make An Eel." The audience fell over hysterically, then gasped to see Colin's hands yanking out of a tank a long, black, slimy creature which he began to flick about like an old twenty-mule-team skinner gone mad. He swished the wriggling sea serpent in the face of a Mrs. Hattie Richardson, an octogenarian from Ardmore, Pa., who cowered but could not refrain from chuckling. "Don't let this eel frighten you, luv. What is an eel, anyway? Just a garden hose with a nervous condition. A tapeworm that took lessons from Mark Spitz." And Colin bestowed that Bugs Bunny giggle on his auditors for a fourth time.

"Today we're going to take Brother Eel and turn him into a lip-smacking breakfast dish. Now pay close attention, gourmet fans." He flung the eel on the butcher block, grasped a bone-handled knife, and beheaded and betailed the creature with quick, competent slashes. "Ah, Colin, you use that knife better than Jack the Ripper. And if this wasn't an eel but a herring you'd be a regular—now get this—Jack the Kipper."

The kipper joke flipped out one of the women so drastically that she snapped her garter belt, sending a shower of silvery hooks flying over the crowd, reminding one young cameraman, a former Nam veteran, of the flechettes from an antipersonnel bomb.

Colin took the eel, sprinkled it with a handful of Pillsbury, and slyly winked. "See? Pillsbury. How's that for—now get this—flour power?" He then mixed flour and egg yolks, adding a quart of milk, until he had a thick paste. "Well, as the umpire said to Hank Aaron, 'Batter up!'"

One of the matrons gushed, "Oh, Colin, you're a card."

"A card? You mean I'm making—" and the TV personality laid in another of his endearing giggles "—an *ace* of myself?" Another monumental laugh.

"Now, a dash of paprika, a dot of oregano, two dashes of cinnamon, two dots of garlic powder... by George, all these dots and dashes. What is this, a recipe or Morse code?"

Jesus, what a dynamite joke, thought director Levi Flare, ordering a tight shot on Colin's grin that exposed the corruscating white teeth and the sensual mouth. *Carew is a frigging genius. Ain't nothin' gonna stop this boy...*

"Now, we put the whole thing on a toasted bun, and, voila, Eel McMuffin!" He popped it into the oven. "Like this bit of hardware? It's my new microwave oven. By the way, luvs, have you ever seen a microwave?" One lady yelled out yes, foolishly falling into his joke trap. "Then if you saw a micro wave, you must also have seen a house fly and a nylon run!" Though embarrassed, she still rocked with laughter and flashed an adoring glance at this fascinating Englishman.

In view of the mesmerizing effect he had on these women, was it any wonder that Colin Carew's rapier wit, unusual culinary expertise, and that distinctive trademark of a cackle had earned him the sobriquet of "The Giggling Gourmet"? From a humble beginning on a local Philadelphia TV station, his show was now being syndicated on over one hundred outlets from coast to coast under the banner of Liberty Bell and, according to constant rumors in the trade papers, was now attracting the attention of moguls of the three major networks.

For the next fifteen minutes Colin kept the patter going at a nonstop clip, offering recipes for the thickest, creamiest salad dressings this side of Maxim's, chopping, grating, and kneading, and fielding questions about food from the audience which he often answered cleverly with music, another Carew shtick.

"Colin, darling, in my backyard there may be truffles. How do I find them and how do I prepare them?" called out a Mrs. Lipsky from Downingtown, Pa.

His mind clicked, he whispered a song title to Barney Baines, the band responded, and to the tune of an old Bing Crosby favorite he sang:

> *"Just put some pigs on your ground,*
> *And let them root all around,*
> *Then wrap your truffles in creams,*
> *And cream your truffles away!"*

"Brilliant, brilliant!" said Flare to his technical director. "Imagine the razor sharpness of that man's mind!" Not knowing that that "razor sharpness" had been hours and hours in the making, with a bleary-eyed Colin sitting up until dawn writing song parodies to cover every known comestible—and then having to memorize them yet. But so spontaneous did they seem when he tossed them out, seemingly on a moment's notice, that they added to his reputation as the ranking wit of the food field. *Variety*, in particular, tagged him as the Clown of the Calories, the Entertainer of the Edibles, and once the Poultrymen's Association had even honored him at an event they jocularly called a "Fryer's Roast."

The truffle issue nicely solved, Colin extracted a vegetable resembling an onion, and while preparing it he crooned, a la Fred Astaire:

> *"Heaven, I'm in heaven,*
> *As I slice away, the tears run down my cheek,*
> *Here's an onion soup that's bound to make you shriek,*
> *When we're out together dining,*
> *Leek to leek!"*

Lusty applause came from those who held fond memories of those great 1930s musicals; then they howled with delight when Colin did a topper. Holding up a pinch of powder, he giggled, "As long as we're doing Astaire, how can we forget—now get this—Ginger?" And let it drop into the leek soup.

On an unstoppable roll, Colin did his next number on a leg of lamb to the accompaniment of Barney and the boys laying in an Irving Berlin oldie as his musical motif.

> "When I'm tired and I can't sleep,
> I'm in my kitchen sauteeing sheep,
> And I fall asleep,
> Puttin' with mutton!"

For his Jewish fans he flung flour and eggs into his Waring blender and trilled "Someday my *Blintz* Will Come"; spotting a Mrs. Mei-ling Chung visiting from Hong Kong, he quickly assembled the makings of an Oriental dish and used a parody of an old Nat King Cole hit, "They Tried to Sell Us Egg Fu Yung." Taking note of the fact the hunting season was at hand and that he'd received many requests for a Sherwood Forest recipe, he tugged a frozen deer out of the Amana, the great branching horns still affixed to the noble head. "Well, if we have to have a stag party, this is the way." Another wave of laughter. Smartly he skinned and dressed it and soon had it revolving on a spit. "If you'll pardon the expression, what a way to make a buck!" When there was a groan he saved the day by saying ruefully, "Don't blame me for that joke, my luvs. Blame my writer, Alfred Lord *Venison*." So brazen was that retort that it garnered a sustained laugh and standing ovation. Perspiring heavily, Colin gave Barney the signal for the sign-off music and ended with his usual "comes from the heart" poem.

The stage went completely dark, except for three strategically and dramatically placed pools of light (an old shtick he'd lifted from the Schnozz, Jimmy Durante) and as he moved from circle to circle he said in a voice he'd lifted from Richard Burton:

> "Au revoir, my luvs, and a fond toodle-oo,
> I hope I've showed you a thing or two,

Some saucy sauces, a bit of mirth,
Some gastric delights from all over the earth.
Don't count those calories, why be a dunce?
Eat all you want; you only live once!
So 'til we meet again on some other day,
Pip, pip, and cheerio, from the Giggling Gourmet."

Standing in that last circle of light, he looked intensely into the camera and said in a hoarse yet tender tone, "Goodnight, Mrs. Succotash, wherever you are." The lights went out, the audience went wild. From the darkness they heard a farewell giggle. One woman who in her teens had swooned for Sinatra's bent notes at the old Paramount Theatre did the same thing when she heard that giggle. Toppled on her face, drooling from a wet mouth: "Oh, Cohn, Cohn...

The others charged to the stage hoping for a final glimpse, now that the taping had concluded. He rewarded them with a reappearance and they swarmed about him begging for an item of clothing, a hanky, a comb. Many shouted, "We only love you, Colin! Betty Crocker is a crock and Julia is just Child's play compared to you!" One even tearfully offered him a Hebrew National salami to be autographed.

"Dynamite," Levi Flare said again, shaking his head in disbelief. He turned to the group of grinning Liberty Bell executives who had inched in to watch the last few minutes from the booth. "You've got a goldmine, Mr. Hamilton. That son-in-law of yours is... but why am I telling you? You know what you've got."

Foster Hamilton, president of the sprawling complex, returned a grin. "Yup. And I haven't even told Colin about this yet." He patted a bulky envelope in the breast pocket of his Brooks Brothers suit. Blair McNeil, Hamilton's vice-president, his own visage enlivened by a fierce grin of monetary anticipation, commented, "Chief, you'd better make sure you've got him tied up for the next thirty years." A bottle of Dewar's was passed about, each exec taking a hefty hit, each chiming in with more late-breaking data about increased fan mail (now thirty thousand letters a week), more approaches from far-flung stations to carry the show, an offer from Random House for a Giggling Gourmet cookbook, a Capitol Records LP which would highlight Colin's food songs.

Only one face in that boisterous bunch was devoid of the exhilaration pervading the booth. It was a craggy face filled with sharp angles, shadowy hollows, resting on a magnificently proportioned body containing great bunching muscles, firm pectorals, a narrow waist, all covered by a black turtle-necked sweater and tight black ski pants with white piping running from the belt line to the ankles. He was Romaine LeLane, the sixty-five-year-old physical marvel who conducted for the same organization an early morning health show predicated on sensible dieting, mystic meditation, and a regimen of vigorous body-building through intensive workouts, all of which had earned him the name of The Exerciser.

Now Flare called out to the women still milling about near the stage, "Hey, gals, you really ought to hang around. We'll be taping another production in about ten minutes, and our next star would love to have a live, enthusiastic audience."

The eyes of Romaine LeLane seemed to brighten with hope as he saw the ladies pause. He heard a few comments buzzing throughout the studio—"Hey, Marge, a free show!" and "Rosalie, if we go home now all we gotta do is make dinner." But when Flare said in a voice brimming with insincerity, "It's Liberty Bell's biggest star, that grand old favorite, The Exerciser, and he'll be glad to show you all how to get rid of those sagging tummies," a chorus of boos and catcalls exploded—"No thanks!" "That old has-been?" "LeLane is a pain"—and they bolted out en masse, some still dreaming of cornering the Giggling Gourmet in the parking lot, perhaps even licking the Carnauba Wax off the hood of his car.

LeLane discerned under the bogus smiles of Hamilton, McNeil, and the others pity, even contempt, but trouper that he was he strode out of the control booth on his powerful legs in a brisk walk down the hall to Studio Two. As he moved toward the performing area he commenced his usual battery of limbering-up exercises—a few deep kneebends, twenty-five simple cartwheels, sixty pushups, one hundred jumping jacks—and then, feeling he was loose enough, bounded on stage. The stagehands were striking the $100,000 Giggling Gourmet set, its sinks, racks, plush rugs, drapes, and walls; and LeLane fell into the spirit of things by picking up the eight-hundred-pound Amana freezer and carrying it to the prop room so that his own set could be assembled. And it was a simple one: a lone sweat-stained floor mat, a few rusty barbells, a Swedish box. The ten-piece band that had played for Carew was gone. For The Exerciser there would be only Miss Hepzibah Beeler, a superannuated spinster who played the wheeziest Wurlitzer organ this side of the Langhorne, Pa., Rollerdrome. In LeLane's mighty, cholesterol-free heart was a raging bitterness. Once *he* had been the kingpin of Liberty Bell, carried by a hundred markets from Maine to California, with a ten-piece band of his own, fan clubs who poured out a thousand letters a day, famous gymnasts from all over the world guesting on his show (Olga Rotgut, the Russian teen tumbler... Bronko Nagasaki, the Japanese weight-lifter... Muhammud Sally, a black Muslim girl turned champion prizefighter) and he had held his own with all of them.

But the Spartan values he had exemplified on TV had fled in the face of the hedonism sweeping the nation, the world. People no longer wanted to eat and exercise sensibly on a planned, regular basis. Today it was starve yourself, then go on a binge. Crash diet, then double malted milks, then back to the crash diet. Worse, they had begun to follow Colin Carew, the Pied Piper of Pastry, the Gastronomical Guru, down the road to flabbiness; Carew with his obscene ten-thousand-calorie desserts, his lewd cream pies, his positively pornographic crêpes and frappés, his Eiffel Tower of a strawberry shortcake.

No matter. The Exerciser had his quest in life and would carry on nevertheless. Pasting a smile on his rocky face that he did not feel inwardly, he began his opening spiel to the bored, yawning cameramen while Miss Beeler thumped away energetically at the only tune she knew, "The Skaters' Waltz." "Good morning, girls. Today we're going to firm up those flaccid arms, so down on the floor and one and two and one and two and . . and that awesome body began its love affair with the canvas.

All over the Delaware Valley, a million remote controls were jabbed by as many TV-watching housewives, who quickly deserted "The Exerciser" for the newest Chuck Barris quiz show, "The Raping Game." "O.K., Cindy," said the toothy emcee, Blink Farthingale, to the leggy airline stewardess, "do you want to be raped by Bachelor Number One, our bonded psycopath just released yesterday from Camarillo; or Bachelor Number Two, our schoolyard candy salesman and pervert from Encino, California; or Bachelor Number Three, our New York subway degenerate who won the coveted Mr. Flasher award?"

"Gee, Blink, I can't make up my mind. They all sound so attractive."

In the penthouse on the fourth floor, Foster Hamilton sat at his genuine Colonial desk, the same piece of furniture that old Ben Franklin allegedly had taken the French ambassador's wife upon, looked at the wall-sized monitor on which LeLane was now working his right knee against his left shoulderblade—"One and two and one and two"— and sighed, "Boring, boring. Poor old bastard." Then felt a surge of guilt. That poor old bastard had made him rich many years ago when Liberty Bell was naught but a small two-floor walkup in center city, Foster operating not out of a sumptuous suite but a tiny room packed with cans of kinescopes and soggy cigarette butts. At that time Foster Hamilton way Liberty Bell literally, the sole cameraman, director, writer, time salesman, bookkeeper, and janitor.

Then one day a splendidly constructed fellow from the West Coast had come in with an idea for an exercise show. Something had ignited in Hamilton's brain. Why not show this gorgeous hunk of man on a medium surfeited by femininity, Lucy in a gown, Loretta Young in a gown, Milton Berle in a gown? The hunch had paid off, and LeLane had rocketed to instant popularity. Each pushup had pushed another thousand dollars into the Liberty Bell coffers and enabled him to launch the mighty syndication organization that he now governed from the penthouse, second in scope only to the major nets themselves. And with it had come marriage to a Bala Cynwyd socialite, the debutante of the season, Cobina Bala-Goola, a lovely daughter, and a fifty-room mansion. Then when tragedy struck and Cobina died in a strange accident, he threw himself harder into his work, becoming a hundred-millionaire in just a few years. Yes, he owed so much to the oldtimer now twisting himself into a Philadelphia pretzel (without the mustard) on the floor of Studio Two. But, dammit, old Romaine really was boring, so he killed the monitor and watched the picture diminish to a tiny pearl drop of a dot. To his son-in-law, who had changed into an orange pullover and fawn-colored slacks, he said, "Have a drink, Colin?"

"Yes, sir," said Colin briskly. "As we say in the soda business—now get this—I could drink Canada Dry." And Hamilton guffawed. Even offstage his son-in-law could not suppress that supple wit.

"Should we have that eel for lunch?"

"Not on your life," Colin said. "That crap is all right for my worshipping ladies, but as for me it's four ounces of lean Chateaubriand, a small tossed salad, and a glass of skimmed milk. If I ate all that bloody swill I was pushing on the telly I'd look like Robert Morley."

"Good thinking," said Hamilton, touching his gold Ronson to the tip of a foot-long Havana. "I'll have the same," and he had his secretary place a call to the takeout counter at the Marriott Lodge. Hamilton took a puff and looked his son-in-law straight in the eye. "Colin, it's no secret to you that I never liked you. Frankly, I considered you the rankest sort of opportunist, snatching away a rich man's daughter when she was in Europe far from her father's leavening restraints. I admit I treated both of you rather badly, but, lad, you've shown me the old get-up-and-go, the kind of drive I had myself when I made my pile. And so after we have a little lunch, I've got a surprise for you... a rich dessert."

"I don't go for rich things."

"But you married my daughter, didn't you?" Hamilton was not above a little humor himself. "No, Cohn, this isn't for the tummy, but for the old bank account." He passed the letter to Colin, who read it quickly, then fell back heavily in the magnificent Chippendale.

"My God."

"That's right, son. NBC wants you to star in a big prime-time Christmas special, and if the numbers and critical acclaim are whammo, it could lead to your very own series on network TV. It's a hell of a format that draws on your basic strengths, your charm, your matchless expertise in all things comestible, your fantastic sense of humor; and all of this will be beefed up... if you'll pardon the food pun"—Colin giggled; he'd file *that* one away for future use on the air—"by a slew of Follies-type chorines to be called the Gourmettes, plus the biggest guest stars. Imagine a ten-minute segment with you and Tennessee Ernie, eating country food and doing country songs together."

"Tennessee Ernie?" Colin's eyes flashed, his mouth spread into a wide, knowing grin. "I've got it. Here's what we sing:

> *"You eat sixteen buns,*
> *And whatta yuh get?*
> *A little bit fatter,*
> *From the buns that you et,*
> *St. Peter, if you wonder where I must go,*
> *I get my buns from the A & P sto'."*

"That's it, beautiful!" And Hamilton rose to impulsively hug his goldmine. "Then maybe we get you and Carroll O'Connor together in another segment..."

"Way ahead of you, Dad. We go to the kitchen set, make meathead pie, dingbat dumplings, and wash it all down with Coon-Aid!"

"Sensational! This special will make the top ten or I don't know my business. And the beauty of it is, Colin, that we do the whole hour at Liberty Bell, which keeps the production money right here in the City of Brotherly Love—and this is one Philadelphia brother who loves money. Of course, that means I'm going to clear the decks around here in preparation for that long-running series I know we'll get out of the special. Which means more expensive sets, better technicians, more promotion, which in turn means I'm going to cut out anything that isn't making money for Liberty Bell. We're going for all the marbles, and we've got no room for deadwood."

"What gets dropped, Dad?"

Hamilton already had his pointer in hand and pressed a button which sent a chart sliding down from the ceiling. "Here, our entire lineup of shows. As you can see, this upward line represents your own show, hottest thing we've got. More than a hundred markets and still rising. Now," and he pointed to another line, " 'The Afternoon at the Zoo,' with our host, Bwana Banana, the great black hunter. When you're operating out of Philly you gotta throw a few crumbs to the ghetto. It's in eighty cities, cheap to produce 'cause we do it right here at the Philly zoo, and the only real expense is the cost of shoveling. Sometimes guest hippos can be overexpressive. That stays. So does 'Sassafrass Street,' our kiddie show—seventy-five markets. Parents love it because we take the sex-education pressure off them and let our adorable puppets explain it. When Punch and Judy do a Masters and Johnson it's a helluva thing to watch." He went down the list of other shows, each holding its own in anywhere from fifty to seventy markets: "Lib and Let Lib," the popular show for the emancipated woman; "Sunshine Seminar," a 6 A.M. college of television, which so far had graduated five hundred brain surgeons, three thousand lawyers, and one Mafia chieftain, who upon achieving his degree muscled in and took over the show.

"Ah." Foster Hamilton gave a sour look. "Here's our weak sister—our strong man."

Colin nodded. He also knew.

"Yup," said Hamilton, "Romaine LeLane. Dwindled to twenty-five markets, mostly in areas where there's a distinct lack of conspicuous consumership, places like St. Petersburg, Sarasota, Sun City, Artery Valley. Those cardiacs don't buy Cadillacs, son, not on social security. Sure, a few old dames still think he's a sex symbol, but so what? You pull in the gravy accounts, the big national stuff, the auto sponsors, the sex-appeal toothpastes, but all LeLane gets are those people who offer the Hundred Golden Hits of Jan Savitt, vocals by Bon-Bon, $4.98 for the LP, $9.98 for the cartridge, or those $1.25 laxatives like Reamo—'When nature isn't working fast, try Reamo for that healthy blast.'"

"Have you told him yet?"

"No, and that's going to be damn tough to do, but I'm sure he's gotten the hint from little things we're doing."

Colin could well imagine what those little things were. First the star taken off the dressing-room door, then the door taken off the dressing room, then the star bodily carried out of the dressing room, his final checks made out to "To whom it may concern." A cold, unsentimental business, and, thank God, he was bound for the top and not on a vertiginous slide to oblivion.

They shook hands warmly, and Colin walked out of the penthouse, elevatored to the ground floor, stood in the wings long enough to see Romaine LeLane, that remarkable body still in play, intoning "One and two and one and two" with now even Miss Beeler sound asleep at the organ, which she had put on automatic pilot and which continued to grind out "The Skaters' Waltz." For Romaine LeLane, The Exerciser, the waltz would soon end.

two

Colin pointed his Mercedes 450 SL into the driveway, swerving a bit to avoid squashing Sihanouk, the imperious Siamese cat who belonged to the Rosenblatts next door, the dreams he had been entertaining all through the trip up I-95 to Levittown still skittering around in his brain. Now the projected one-hour special, his ticket to permanent fame and fortune, was taking shape: Christmas night at ten; a dulcet announcer's voice, "This is an NBC color presentation," the peacock appearing, its tail fanning out to reveal the rainbow hues, then (oh clever touch!) Colin appearing in animation to grasp the bird by the neck, flick it and fling it into a bubbling cauldron while a cheery voice (Ed MacMahon? Hugh Downs?) cried out, "Welcome to the Giggling Gourmet Variety Hour and now he-e-e-e-e-r-r-r-r-e's Colin!"

Truly he had come a long way from his mean origins in London's sooty Cheapside section of the East End. He had been born the scrawny son of Benjy and Bertha Pickles, two Cockneys who had never been more than a millimeter away from starvation. Dad and Mum, he of the tiny, wiry body, she of the creamy complexion and incredible breasts, were buskers, smalltime street entertainers, who stood outside the grand West End theatres singing their shopworn little ditties to the disdainful amusement of the playgoing toffs and their bejeweled ladies who haughtily tossed a shilling. In those days he was known as Alfie Pickles and by the age of five he was right next to Dad (rarely next to Mum; those monstrous globes making propinquity hard to achieve), dancing his little steps and holding out his grubby cap for the showers of coins that sometimes never came. During the London Blitz there were terrible nights when the Pickleses, like so many other Londoners, huddled in underground shelters, quaking with each explosion, listening to Winnie's gravelly voice on the radio bringing its immortal message, "Never before have so many and so much done so much for so few and so many and so much and so little and so never before have so many..." to which Benjy Pickles commented wryly, "The old boy's been at the brandy decanter again. It may not be our finest hour, but it sounds like his."

Then tragically all those damp nights in the shelter took their toll and ravaged Benjy's malnourished little body until he succumbed to chilblain. ("An amazing case," a Dr. Smedley Huntoon was later to say in *The Lancet*, the British journal of medicine. "The poor beggar had ten chils to every blain, definitely a medical first.") So Alfie and Mum were left alone, but not before the boy took Dad's dying words to heart:

"Stay in show business, Alfie lad. It's been good to Mum and me. Learn your songs and your jokes and somehow the good Lord will see you through."

When the bluebirds came back over the White Cliffs of Dover and the lights went on again all over the world and the nightingales sang once more in Berkeley Square, Alfie, now seven, went into show biz with a vengeance. He and Mum got together a little act and began touring the small vaudeville houses of the United Kingdom. Mum would do a medley of risqué barmaid songs, including "In the Tower of London So Dark and Full of Dread, Is Where Anne Boleyn Gave King Henry Some Head." Toward the end of their turn little Alfie would appear in a toga to win the hearts of the working-class audiences by reciting Shakespeare, for even at that tender age his unerring ear had picked up and was able to make his mouth mimic the Old Vic accents of the Oliviers and the Gielguds.

In addition, Alfie began to pay close attention to the many comedians who appeared on the bill, copying their routines, their joke rhythms and he even purloined his eventually-to-be-famous trademark from a Welsh comedian, Phil S. Diller, who made bad jokes somehow more endurable by inserting a covering giggle over the punchlines.

But their stipends in show business were scant, so the Pickleses were forced to moonlight by working in pubs and restaurants, Mum as a waitress, Alfie as a busboy. It was in these establishments that the observant youngster began to absorb the knowledge of food preparation. By the time Alfie was eighteen he was no mean hand at either a recitation from a Shaw play or a beef stroganoff.

By now Mum was too old to continue her career; thankfully she moved in with a second-rate vaudevillian, Hubert Orkney, whose specialty act was squeezing balloons and making melodies from the escaping air. One look at Mum's own balloons convinced Hubert it would be love at first squeeze. Many a night was spent in their run-down flat, his fingers desperately trying to draw the glorious notes of Mozart's Symphony No. 41 in C from Mum's equally glorious Maidenform in 44-D.

On his own, Alfie pursued his goal of stardom, working as a comedian-emcee in Soho strip joints, further refining his own style, stealing material shamelessly from other funnymen. Convinced that Alfie Pickles was not destined to be a household word, he even filched a new name, one that smacked of theatrical royalty, Colin Carew, plus the voices of Richardson, Redgrave, and Laughton.

But there were dry periods too, and thankfully he had the restaurant experience to fall back on. But now he was beyond the busboy level, enjoying new status as a short-order cook, even a chef. It was then that he made two rather astute observations that would cinch his future. He noticed that middle-class American tourists (A) genuflected to anything they considered "class," especially a British accent, even from a lowly lift operator, and (B) went into paroxysms of delight over anything in the food line more sophisticated than Philadelphia scrapple on toasted Wonder Bread points. One day he would weld these two into a powerful force for self-aggrandizement.

Then in 1972 he met Camille Hamilton, a guest at the Mayfair Hotel, where he was working as a maitre d'. He moved about smartly in his striped trousers and cutaway coat, offering little tea sandwiches of watercress and cucumber, drawing sighs from the many unattached American schoolteachers on holiday. More than one of these educators yielded to this polished, presentable Englishman and ended up in his digs on Cheshire Mews, proving through nights of wild, unrestrained lovemaking the merit in that old adage, "Teacher is the best experience."

A friend, Lloyd Barrington, the hotel desk clerk, had whispered that the smashing Miss Hamilton, she of long straight blonde hair, wasp waist, slender shapely legs, and full breasts, was an heiress to an American TV fortune; so Colin set his cap for the girl. But he discovered that Miss Hamilton, no matter how beguiling his approach, had a supreme disinterest in food, thus accounting for that superb 105-pound figure. He also noticed there was a sadness about the girl that could not be dented by his stream of badinage.

But in Hyde Park one day as he took his constitutional, he came upon Miss Hamilton, a fetching sight in her loose flowing smock, standing in front of an easel upon which was a canvas of an old flower lady she had been painting. "Oh, darn, there's something missing and I just don't know what."

Colin, who had caught a quick glance at the work, knew what, and emitting his most charming giggle, swaggered over with the manliness of a Michael Caine, whose walk he had copied from *The Ipcress File*.

"May I?" He smiled, took the brush from her hand, made two dots and a curved line. "Perhaps this will do it."

"Of course!" The frown fled her delicate face. "That's what it needed—two eyes and a mouth. Funny how one misses the little details. You're so clever!"

With a modest shrug (which he had copied from John Mills) he sat next to her and patted her arm. "Oh, no, my dear. Actually you had it all, the perspective, the angle, the feel, the mood, the richness of texture and color. My adding the eyes and mouth was just the icing on the cake, the capping of a masterpiece."

This inevitably led to the sharing of his basket lunch, a long serious discussion about the world of art she was so eager to affiliate with, and matters of a more personal nature. Her gloom, it seemed, had been caused by the death of her mother, Cobina, whose mountainous breasts had been her undoing. It was her wont to visit Connie Mack Stadium, where she and her husband, Foster, great fans of the futile Phillies, had a season's box behind the home-team dugout. But due to an urgent conference one afternoon, Mr. Hamilton had been unable to attend, so she went alone. Bored with the isolation of the box seat, she had a strange desire to see the game like the common fan did. So she wandered all the way to the upper left-field stands and took an empty seat. In the fourth inning Ron Santo of the Cubs drove a high liner to deep left, and the excited Mrs. Hamilton stood up to catch the homerun ball. Alas, her great mammaries shifted forward too quickly as she bent for the spheroid and suddenly pulled her over the railing, out of the upper deck, and she fell sixty feet, landing upon the unfortunate left-fielder. He survived somehow; she did not.

And so the grieving Camille had come to Europe to forget, to lose herself in her art. During that first long talk in the park with this young man, who seemingly had been able to unlock a heart weighted with sorrow, she unbent enough to modestly show Colin some of her other work— her curious portrait of the world-famous clock, Big Ben, to which she had unthinkingly added a watch strap and the word BENRUS. All of her art seemed to be a trifle off-center, but he didn't have the heart to laugh, so earnest was she.

The relationship grew. Miss Hamilton became Camille, then the more intimate Camy, and this ultimately took them to his room where by candlelight he removed her pert, stylish Mary Quant mini-skirt, proving again that he was the biggest Quant-man in London. In three weeks he had cut into her soul like O. J. Simpson through right tackle, and she was irrevocably, unalterably, insanely his.

When his own vacation came, the lovers hired a stubby little Morris Minor and wended their way leisurely through the countryside, stopping at such quaint historical sites as Stratford-on-the-Avon, Avon-on-the-Doorbell, and Munching-on-the-Fritos, each day the bond more solid, the promises more passionate. But even in the midst of lovemaking he noticed her reserve. She would never emit anything more vulgar than "darn" or "golly," a trait he found rather appealing in this day of modern girls spouting profanities.

To Cohn, what had started out as a coldblooded run at her fortune had now turned to a deep affection. Why not marry this lissome maid from Philadelphia with her sweetness, innocence and seemingly inexhaustible BankAmericard? Perhaps through her he could reach the prominence he so justly deserved.

On a misty night in Devon, that terrible spot where Holmes and Watson had tracked the monster of the moor, they rousted a cranky, withered justice of the peace from his bed and said the vows. And with the legendary Hound of the Baskervilles (who had stopped tearing out the throat of a passing shepherd long enough to place a bloody paw on the marriage contract), acting as witness (who else was available in Devon at 3 in the morning?), the union was sealed.

Naturally when the lovers called Foster Hamilton with the good news, the tycoon had exploded, his scathing invectives melting the Trans-Atlantic Cable, forcing the British to send frogmen down to repair the sundered line. "You've been had, dammit! All right, baby, you're hitched, but keep that money-hungry Limey out of my sight. He's not getting any lendlease from Foster Hamilton."

Camille had stiffened and displayed the old moxie. "Oh, daddy, go to perdition"—a rather shocking word for her—and clicked off. "Well, at least, let's meet your side of the family."

But Colin had somehow talked her out of that get-together. Firstly, how would Camille take to Mum with her earthy, bawdy talk? He would be ashamed to have his true background revealed. And then there was the matter of Mum's boggling protuberances. Would they not remind Camille of her own mother's gigantic globes, the cause of her death? He felt guilty about ducking the meeting, but pledged he'd arrange one in the future and promptly forgot about it.

Then Camille predictably got homesick for the Delaware Valley and they decided to return to America.

But having no desire to live in a fetid Philadelphia apartment, Camille sank her trust fund into the purchase of the Clubber on Dovedroppings Lane. She worked in a little art supplies store in the Levittown Shopping Center, making $75 a week and still painting on the side, her faces, thanks to Colin, now containing the proper number of eyes, noses, and ears, but backsliding in other anatomical areas—human hands that were all thumbs, literally, and feet with webbed toes. Colin was doing his best to bring a few bucks into the house. He played occasional one-nighters at Philadelphia's many private social clubs, where he did his medley of impersonations and his Cockney songs, and jested with the patrons. They made friends with the Rosenblatts at 56 Dovedroppings, Arnold the renowned designer for the world-famous Bounce-Arama Mattress Company, and his wife, Rona, with her lush physique, whom he used as his enthusiastic test pilot in fervent nights of research and development. On the other side, at 52 Dovedroppings, were Hank and Helen Henderson, he a bank vice president, she a Garden Club chairwoman, who underscored their ultraconservative politics by referring to their powder room as the John Birch.

In mid-1973 Colin's big break came, but he made it happen himself. Early one evening, he turned on Channel

48 and there was a high-busted old dowager, Henrietta McKeever, droning on in a flutey voice about the proper way to marinate chuck steak. My God, he thought, what banality, what dullness! This woman had all the personality of a Sominex tablet. If she had been on CBS that famed eye would have closed ten minutes ago. Why were all American cooking shows—and he had seen many on both commercial and educational TV—so damnably boring? In a flash of genius he saw where his destiny lay. He called up Channel 48 and conned his way into an appointment the next afternoon with a Mr. Poindexter, the program director, who as luck would have it was fed up to his ultra-high frequency signal with the turgid Mrs. McKeever, whose last Nielsen Rating showed she was two points under the all-night test pattern.

Colin, always a master at creating by the seat of his pants, outlined what he thought a cooking show should be. "By God, sir, if you want to appeal to the women, let a handsome man be the host."

On a crisp fall night Colin Carew stepped before an American TV camera for the first time. "Good evening, my luvs. I'm Colin Carew from jolly old Blighty, so whether you're clad in a swimsuit or nightie, just stick with the man who cooks cold or hot, and I'll soon have you all going right to pot!" And with a ladle he banged the large Revere ware copper vessel. "On this show, my luvs, I don't do rimshots, I do—now get this—potshots." And gave out his first mirth-provoking giggle.

The handful of technicians who had greeted this newcomer with insouciance doubled up with laughter, spurring Colin on to even wilder turns of phrase. All the shtick he had picked up in the nightclubs and restaurants was coming together, and soon he was slicing his merry way through palate-enticing recipes for smoked salmon a la Glasgow (which he cheerfully termed Lox Lomond), topping each outrageous pun with the infectious giggle he had borrowed so long ago from that vaudevillian.

"Bejesus and begorrah, Mr. Poindexter," said the old Irish cleaning lady in his office, "this new bucko of yours is a regular Giggling Gourmet."

"What?" Poindexter rose out of his chair. "What did you say?"

"I said, Giggling Gourmet, bejesus, begorrah, and Gypo Nolan, what did ye do with the twenty pounds?" Exhausting her Hibernian repertoire, she shuffled off.

The rest was history. In ten weeks he had shot up to the top in Philadelphia and one night a contrite Foster Hamilton drove up to Levittown and made his peace. Though still a trifle wary of his new son-in-law, he was smart enough not to let emotions becloud his good business sense. He offered a bigger and better version of the Giggling Gourmet on Liberty Bell syndication for $3,000 a week. "And while you're at it, kids, there's plenty room for the two of you at my house."

Colin shrewdly refused. "No, Mr. Hamilton, my audience is that middle-class housewife who's looking for a touch of sophistication. By living here in this very heart of the middle-class I keep my fingers on the pulse of my viewers."

So they remained in Levittown, but the ratty Volkswagen with the Stevenson-Sparkman bumpersticker was replaced by the Mercedes, and Camille refurbished the Clubber and bought the art supplies store, turning it into a boutique and art gallery she inventively called Camille's Boutique and Art Gallery, where she sold her own works at vastly inflated prices. True, there were some patrons who would quibble at her thematic approach; for instance, her rendition of Gainsborough's Blue Boy was painted totally in brown, but owning a painting that had been executed (even murdered) by the wife of the Giggling Gourmet became the ultimate in snob appeal.

With a turn of the key he switched off the eight-cylinder engine and the flashback, and he walked into the rec room she had transformed into a studio. She was on her knees in front of her unfinished masterwork, a sculpture of the god Thor. "Darling," he said, kissing that sweet mouth, "use clay. I don't think Playdough will hold up in the kiln."

"Oh, Colin, you're so right, as usual. Dinner will be ready in five minutes. Louisiana has really been cooking up a storm all afternoon."

He led her to a soft living-room chair, poured a diet cola for both, and unloaded his staggering good news. She listened intently, then lapsed into a gloomy silence. "What's wrong, Camy?"

"It's what I've always feared. Isn't it bad enough that I die a thousand deaths from jealousy at the thought of those women, those food groupies of yours, clawing at you every day in the studio? Now there'll be millions of them all over the world; you'll be on promotional tours, do guest shots in Hollywood; and sure as God made little green apples—"

"For which I have a splendid recipe," he broke in chuckling. "Ever taste my God's little green apple pie?"

"Sure as He did, one of those starlets will bed you down like a scoop of tuna in a bower of escarole. Oh, Colin, isn't local success enough? We're so happy here with our house, our friends."

"Luv, your old man doesn't want to be just a big fish in a little pond. Trust me. It'll be smashingly super for the both of us." He lit a cigarette and puffed out a curl of smoke. "One thing bothers me, Camy. That special has got to be double dynamite. Ox Bernaise and panther pudding are passable enough for local syndication, but if I'm to stand up before thirty million souls and make an impact in the ratings I've got to come up with something wild, far-out, that'll have every critic raving. But what in heaven's name is left? I've gone through every fancy dish in the book. Whale parmigian', sweet and pungent porcupine, blue-assed rhesus monkey in tartar sauce..."

"I'm sure you'll come up with something, dear," she said, sipping her soda. At that moment Louisiana, their recently acquired maid, stuck her great black head, wrapped in a bandanna, into the doorway and trumpeted through legions of gold teeth, "Come 'n' git it, y'all."

They sat down to a steaming dish of Jambalaya crawfish pie, topped by Lousiana's intestine-eroding hot sauce, which Colin had quickly deduced she was getting from leftover atomic wastes at the Hanford plant. A genuine find, this Louisiana, Colin knew. Like so many other impoverished blacks she had come up from the sleepy bayous of her home state to seek a better way of life in the more affluent north. On the day of her interview Colin, his hyperactive comedy mind ever moving, had not been able to resist saying, "So you're from Louisiana, eh? How's bayou?" To which Louisiana had replied with profound dignity, "Sheeeeeeyit..."

If Louisiana had removed her bandanna, peasant blouse, and full flowered skirt to reveal herself in the altogether, she would have presented the picture of a Grambling University linebacker, so massive was her 250-pound body, with its great black bowling balls of buttocks resting on two piano legs. This amazing strength had stood her in good stead back home, where frequently she had rescued drowning alligators by giving them mouth-to-mouth resuscitation with great gusts of air from her powerful lungs, a process she called Gator-aid. Despite that bulk she moved fluidiy throughout the Carew household completing the cleaning and cooking chores in less than an hour a day.

Soon she became a neighborhood favorite with her deep chuckle and folksy humor, and more than one Country Clubber resident had tried to lure her away from the Carews, but she focused an overwhelmingly maternal feeling on Camille, whom she called "mah sweet, tiny chile," that precluded the possibility of her moving on. To Camille, who often missed her own mother more than she cared to admit, Louisiana's great warm presence was a source of comfort.

Everyone loved her, with one exception—Bandini the gardener, who never lost an opportunity to hurl in a racial slur when she appeared on the lawn. One day, after a particularly nasty shouting match, Louisiana went into Camille's studio, deftly fashioned a clump of Playdough into an effigy of Bandini, mumbled an ancient obeah curse, and thrust a hatpin into its groin. Outside, Bandini doubled up with excruciating pain, and as a byproduct found himself quite sterile.

After dinner Louisiana waddled upstairs to her large, calico-curtained bedroom to camp in front of her twenty-five-inch RCA, nibble a few pounds of pralines, and watch the Waltons show the world what fun things Depression, hunger, and poverty really were.

While Camille worked on her sculpture of Thor, Colin interrupting to say the teeth should be moved *inside* the mouth, he pored over several dozen cookbooks by James Beard, Duncan Hines, and *The New York Times,* shaking his head disconsolately from time to time. Not a grabber in the bunch, except possibly the kangaroo a la mode with the ice cream in the pouch—but, Lord knew, that had been done to death. When the phone rang he was already down to the rock bottom, recipes for cookies made from Kellogg's Rice Krispies.

"Colin?" The voice fought through a field of crackling static. "It's me, old man, Sir Roderick Pish-Teppie on the horn from jolly old Calcutta, where cholera is king."

"Roderick, you old fig!" Colin laughed. "How fabulous to hear from you." And he remembered with fondness the visit of the famed explorer-archeologist to his show many weeks back. What a session that had been, old Roderick demonstrating how to make tasty dishes from the kind of fauna to be found on the great Serengeti Plain of Africa, the water-buffalo-chip cookies, the rhinoburgers, the baboon bread. "What's shaking, you old peripatetic bounder?"

"I'm about to embark upon a rather interesting sojourn for *National Geographic,* old fellow. They've commissioned me to lead an expedition to the very summit of Everest, where a Japanese team was lost last month, but not before they radioed in news of startling prehistoric finds, including some rather obscure foods that should intrigue a chap in your fine."

"Such as?" Cohn's heart skipped a beat.

"Yak waffles."

"Yak waffles? How devastating! I've simply got to join you."

A voice broke in. "That will be a thousand rupees for the next three minutes, sair."

"Righto, operator. Now listen, Colin, I knew I could hook you. What say we rendezvous at the Hilton Nepal on the twenty-fifth and we'll give it a rum go."

"As long as the rum holds out, I'll go," Colin jibed, sending his storied wit halfway around the world. "See you on the twenty-fifth. Love to Babs and the young ones." He hung up, his spirit renewed. Sir Roderick's call had been manna from heaven. (And, incidentally, how *did* one make manna from heaven? God only knew.) What a stunning opportunity to pluck from the recesses of forbidden Tibet a dish probably never before tasted by Western palates, and to actually expose it on that Christmas special. Yak waffles! What a coup for the Giggling Gourmet! The entire country would be buzzing about it over their morning Yuban.

Again fate had served him a soft lob over the net and he was ready to put it away with a service ace for matchpoint. And how great it would be to slog along with Sir Roderick, as good a climber as ever drove a piton into the face of a cliff, the only man who had ever scaled the Matterhorn at Disneyland. To Camille he said, "What say to a Tibetan jaunt?"

"Oh, Colin, you know I can't. Things are booming at the boutique. I've got to finish my commissioned portrait of the Rosenblatt boy for his Bar Mitzvah next week and I'm having a problem finding a spot for the cross..."

"Star of David, dear."

"Oh, yes, my love. And the library wants my Thor in time for the dedication of the new wing, and I have only a week to do that mural for the bank building lobby, which is rather demanding because I'm delving into a new medium, Kemtone and a roller. You go, darling, and do all that manly stuff with Roderick. But if you come back with one of those slinky, almond-eyed vamps I'll..."

"I promise, luv, I won't be Himalaid in the Himalayas," he jested, hugging her hard. He dashed into the bedroom to begin packing, piling into his battered Samsonite luggage the necessities for a trip of this nature: the sealskin parka, the thermal long johns, the heavy woolen gloves, spiked boots and, significantly, the large economy size of Kaopectate.

Whistling merrily he buckled up the bursting bags, eager for that momentous climb to the top of the world. But had Colin Carew known what was waiting for him there, the horror that crouched among the ice storms waiting to be unleashed, to wreak its vile havoc upon that innocent house of happiness at 54 Dovedroppings Lane, he would have gladly passed up Tibet and opened his prestigious special with a seminar on 101 ways to delump oatmeal.

But the horror knew it had hauled in a victim. And the wind outside passed its message: *It's coming... it's coming... it's coming...* And again the frightened animals reacted with madness. A Doberman Pinscher climbed a tree and meowed at the moon, a field mouse popped out of a hole and beat the shit out of a tomcat, seventeen Japanese beetles committed hara-kiri by swarming through an open screen and electrocuting themselves by jumping onto the picture tube of an American-made TV set.

Yes, the horror was getting closer, and there was nothing under the stars that could stop it.

three

In any other place in the world the sight of a muscular, craggy-faced man in black turtle-neck sweater and gym shorts doing a series of rather extreme calisthenics as he moved down the palm-lined street—handstands on the roof of a Lincoln Continental, squeezing a watermelon he had just bought in order to strengthen his wrists and fingers, kicking down a parking meter to keep his calves and quadriceps well toned, or even crouching like the Olympian he once was to yank a fire hydrant out of its cement base to give his pectorals and biceps a good workout—could conceivably have caused a raised eyebrow or two.

But not in Santa Monica, California, whose golden sands play host to that renowned home of bronzed beefcake called Muscle Beach. And what this man was doing was par for the course, for he had been a folk hero in that exclusive preserve of the body beautiful for many years. This was home base for Romaine LeLane, The Exerciser.

He had flown in that morning from Philadelphia after a breakfast meeting with Foster Hamilton. LeLane had eaten just a head of lettuce—Romaine, of course, in proud tribute to his first name—and watched Hamilton wolfing down a distasteful mound of fat-saturated French toast with maple syrup and granulated sugar, heaping platefuls of greasy, starchy sausages, and cup after cup of caffeine-poisoned coffee.

"That garbage will kill you some day, Foster," the old strongman noted to his longtime boss. Correction—ex-boss, because Hamilton gave him the word.

"Romaine, we've come a long way together, but yesterday's show was your last. We're not picking up your option. Got to make room for the new wave. Now Liberty Bell isn't heartless, and I think you'll find this severance check quite generous."

He handed over an oblong strip of green paper which LeLane promptly shoved into his mouth, anything green immediately bringing to mind a low-calorie, leafy vegetable. While the amused Hamilton was writing another check, he thought, it's a good thing I didn't pay him off in bills. He would have thought it was a spinach salad.

Then there was just a farewell kiss from Miss Beeler, her fingers still working over "The Skaters' Waltz," and he rolled up the three-hundred-pound sweat-stained mat and hoisted it onto his back, shoved a barbell under each armpit, and walked the twenty-five miles to Philadelphia International Airport. Dismissal or not, The Exerciser was not about to break training.

"It's Romaine LeLane!" His name was called out by the musclemen and their girls who saw him cartwheeling down the shoreline toward the area covered by volleyball courts, rings, and chinning bars. "Welcome home, old-timer!"

Here they remember, his heart told him. Here they love me. Amd he reached into his pockets and threw them handfuls of powdered nonfat milk as a reward for loyalty.

On this very spot the local boy who had been born the eldest son of two Lesbians, Labia and Lucretia LeLane, had come as a stripling to seek sun and sea and bodily health. His parents had been strongwomen in the LaStrada Circus in Milan, imparting their musculature to their firstborn, who took their genetic gift and tenaciously built it into Herculean dimensions.

The sharp eye of an Olympic track coach spotted him on the sand in 1935, his chest and arms bursting out of his jacket, and immediately entered him in the 1936 games. He amazed even the sullen Nazis with his prowess, hurling the javelin 340 yards, a not inconsiderable feat because there was a two-hundred-pound javelin thrower still attached to it. He won three gold medals at that historic event and could have captured more, but he deliberately let fellow-American Jesse Owens win a few events to humiliate the Nordics and their insane Führer.

LeLane, far deeper into philosophical pursuits than the rest of his fellow strongmen, considered the body more than a mere collection of tissue, muscle, blood, and bone. It was a temple to all that man should be, in his efforts to be Godlike, strong, pure, untainted by foul digestive indiscretions. And in that context The Exerciser waged a lifelong battle against strengthsapping liquor, body-bloating carbohydrates, all of which he considered weapons of a demonic force out to destroy mankind or at least imprison it in San Quentins of fat. Thus he trusted solely organic foods to his system, but only those of a high-protein character. He found favor with wheat germ (and when that was not available he ate diseased wheat) and blackstrap molasses (strap and all), only whole grains, unpasteurized milk, the marrow from beef bones, vegetables grown without pesticides, distilled water (he drank only from Sears Die-Hard batteries).

In his pantheon of idols were Bernarr MacFadden, Charles Atlas, Johnny Weismuller, Herman Brix and, for some odd reason, Popeye the Sailorman, the latter giving him mixed emotions. (Loved the spinach, loathed the pipe.)

And many of these doyens of physicality would be his guests at his beachhouse where they would sit around, arm-wrestle a bit, chew on kelp smeared with Smuckers jellyfish, and quaff large tumblers of iodine wine. (Non-intoxicating and great for internal bleeding.) Once even the circus star, Gargantua, was invited for the weekend, but the great ape was bored by the conversation and went to Sunset Boulevard "to pick up broads."

To LeLane physical weakness was not to be tolerated, and this precept led to the great personal tragedy in his life. He had a younger brother, Parsley LeLane, a 98-pound weakling, for it seemed that Labia and Lucretia had blown it all on Romaine. One day the paper-thin, unmuscled Parsley sat on a blanket with a USC co-ed when a bully swaggered into view and kicked sand in his face. The co-ed urged Parsley to defend his honor, but the lad feared bodily injury. Humiliated, he went to his big brother and asked him to thrash die bully within an inch of his life. Romaine refused. "If you want to be a real man," he said, "you must do it yourself. But I will show you how, disgusting sibling."

And he put Parsley through a crash course of body-building, employing the techniques of dynamic tension, isometrics, isotonics, kung fu, karate, judo and jiu-jitsu. The results were soon evident in the boy's burgeoning physique, which grew ever harder and tauter until his chest began popping the buttons off his Arrow shirts.

But his older brother's fanaticism went a whit too far. He pushed Parsley into a maneuver rarely done in strength and health circles, the Aztec Turnaround, in which the practitioner must curl his hands through his crotch, grasp his buttocks and, utilizing all his muscles, hold his entire body three feet in the air. Parsley, ever anxious to please his big brother, tried it. When he was one foot off the ground in a holding pattern, there was a heart-rending crack and Parsley tumbled to the sand, hideously bent, never to stand straight again. Wisely he dropped out of USC and enrolled at Notre Dame, where they possess an ancient empathy for hunchbacks. Romaine would never forget Parsley's haunted eyes... *"You did this to me"*... and it was a sorrow he would bear all his life.

Now he was swinging on the rings, still evoking the oohs and ahs from the crowd, as good as any man thirty years his junior. But who wanted his talents anymore? Not Liberty Bell, which had deigned to go with Carew and his sauces and creams. He, The Exerciser, was finished.

So he thought.

But there was a dark star looming in his horrorscope and it would steer him into the strangest confrontation of his or any other man's life.

The Pacific Ocean, which had been tipped off by the chatterbox winds, now crashed against the jetty... *It's coming... it's coming... it's coming...* and despite the brilliant sun, The Exerciser was rocked by a chill.

four

Colin met Sir Roderick Pish-Tepple in the bar of the Hilton Nepal, the latter already into his ninth Jack Daniels, roisterous and full of bonhommie, the pockets of his bush jacket crammed with maps and charts and an erotic photo of Dame May Whitty being smothered by Robert Montgomery in a scene from *Night Must Fall*. At the explorer's side was a pint-sized brown man with slanted eyes who wore a lambskin hat and a saffron robe, whom he introduced as their Sherpa guide, Yentzing, "A man who's climbed as many maidens as mountains. My sort of chap, definitely."

Yentzing shook hands solemnly and in his singsong Oriental voice said, "It is written that a journey of a thousand miles must begin with a single step. And if you're going that far, it is not unwise to take a single broad." They nodded at his sagacity and took turns punching him in the mouth.

Outside the bar was the marketplace bustling with other small brown men sliding their toothless gums over chunks of ghee, the rancid buffalo butter; and camel drivers whose great beasts of burden stood parked, their OFF DUTY signs reflected in the sun; and the usual ragtag coterie of American hippies who had come to the Far East to smoke the potent hash that grew freely in the streets. Those already sated with hash were inhaling each other, an even greater high. The lone evidence of modernity was the ubiquitous Baskin-Robbins ice cream franchise, but even here the native flavors dominated—Orange Sherpa, Raspberry Sherpa, Lime Sherpa, and the chocolatey Rocky Burma Road.

Colin's excitement mounted during Sir Roderick's description of the itinerary: First Katmandu, then the jungles, and finally up the glittering sides of Everest to the mysterious cave that the Japanese had found at the summit.

That afternoon they set out and experienced the discomfort of having their faces slashed time and again by the valley's razor grass, which Roderick identified as *Schickus Injectus,* and the indignity of being set upon by that curse of Nepal, the leeches that dropped in showers from the tree limbs to suck their claret. Roderick also identified these scientifically as *agentus William Morrisia.* "These only take ten per cent of your blood," he said reassuringly.

The terrain changed dramatically from lush foliage to sparse lichens and moss as the air grew colder and the party climbed higher. Here where wild Himalayan winds sang "The Wayward Wind" and other Gogi Grant hits, the only sign of life was a passing Abominable Snowman, known as a Yeti, and his wife, a Yetta, the latter whining, "You never take me any place. You just stalk around the mountains in your size twenty-nine-double-E Florsheims, leaving horrifying tracks that scare the shit out of the world, while I have to stay in the cave all day milking the yaks. And, incidentally, buster, I'm not an Abominable Snowwoman, I'm a Snow*person.*" "Oh, God," the husband carped, "ever since Gloria Steinem came through here you've been a pain in the ass."

Thanks to Sir Roderick's superb mountaineering, agility, and the helicopter he had arranged to pick them up at the ten thousand-foot level, they made it to the very top in one day, discovering the frozen Japanese, still strung together on their safety ropes like a charm bracelet of the dead, the Sony shortwave over which they had made their frantic last appeal still operational, even in the subzero temperatures. "They make a splendid product," Sir Roderick conceded, flipping to another station. A voice rattled out, "Hi, chicks and chickies, Chinks and Chinkesses, this is your Far East boss jock, Red Guard, bringing you all the heavy hits from Rangoon to Peking. Before we get to Number Three on the charts, Ho Chi Minh and the Trailblazers doing their big breakout hit with a bullet, a real bullet, 'Thai a Yalu River 'Round the Old Oaktree,' let's sell something. Now I'm sure you all have—or you better have—a copy of the Chairman's Little Red Book to keep you philosophically out of sight. But, man, if you plan to come to downtown Shanghai for a little swinging, you oughta have a copy of the Chairman's Little *Black* Book, with the greatest list of wonton women this side of the Mustang Ranch. And it's only one hundred sen. So if you wanna party with the Party..." When Yentzing began filling out a postcard, they decided to snap off the Sony.

At last, the cave. Brooding. Silent. Cut out of the rock by millions of years of eroding winds.
Yentzing led the way, his torch casting an eerie shadow on the dank walls. Moving further down its tunnel Colin began to spot evidences of early life, skeletons strewn about, piles of fur rags, implements which appeared to be pristine chisels and axes. As they descended deeper into the bowels they came upon a cauldron, and Colin's heart leaped. There it was inside—yak waffles!, obviously kept from decomposing by the rarefied air. Though it was dangerous from a sanitary standpoint, he could not resist taking a mouthful. "Delicious," he exclaimed. "Needs a little Accent to bring out the full glory of the flavor, but delicious nevertheless." Ah, this would be the Rosetta Stone of food!
Meanwhile Roderick poked about on his own, discovered more artifacts, and knelt to assay the content of some round frozen balls he had plucked from a pit. At first he could not identify the material, but when he spied some hieroglyphics scrawled on a nearby wall he knew they might explain the function of this section of the cave. A

master semanticist, Roderick quickly translated and broke into a belly laugh. Now he knew where he was for sure.

"What does it say?"

"It says, 'Guys who write on shithouse walls, roll their shit into little balls; guys who read these lines of wit, eat those little balls of shit.' "

"By Jove," Colin said. "The first graffiti. So here's where it started." Enrapt by all the wondrous findings in this treasure trove of culture, he began to outpace the others in his zeal to discover more. "Careful, Colin!" Sir Roderick called out; but it was too late. He felt a rock giving way, then more, then a slide and he was falling, screaming frantically, until a blow seared his brain and all was darkness.

How long he lay he didn't know, but it was the faint voices of Sir Roderick and Yentzing that stirred him to life. Now they were louder, reverberating off the walls. "Colin, Colin, where are you, lad?"

He felt the back of his head and the knot that had risen when he banged into... into what? He opened his eyes and gasped. Then he found his hands fluttering with fear. "Here, here," he shouted, and thrilled to see the beams of their flashlights. "But mind your step."

His companions threw a rope into the lower level where he had fallen, tied one end to a rock. Now Sir Roderick clambered down to join him.

Yentzing called down. "Worthy sirs, what do you see?"

Colin cupped his hands around his lips. "It's amazing. A dozen dead men, fat and bloated, all seated about a sort of festive table... the first Last Supper. But come and see for yourself."

"Me?" Yentzing's eyes widened and began rolling like deranged marbles. "Down dere wit' all dem dead people? You ain't gonna get me in dere, Missuh Chan." He looked down at his feet. "Snowshoes, do yo' stuff." And he ran out of the cave to the safety of the helicopter.

Strange how men can undergo startling change in the face of fear, Colin thought.

"Amazing," Sir Roderick spoke at last. "These blokes have been so hermetically sealed in this hidden chamber that they didn't fall into dust, but just ossified."

He moved in to make an inspection. The dozen were dressed in the robes and three-cornered hats of mandarin priests. Even in death they appeared to be waiting for some spectral waitress to fill their bowls with the next course. "Here, in the bowls, more yak waffles. And from the size of these chaps I'd say they'd been eating nonstop for a year. It's like looking at twelve barrage balloons out to lunch. God only knows what killed them."

"Maybe this." Colin's flashlight played on something in the rear of the chamber.

It was an idol, sixty feet tall, hewn out of a greenish stone. It sat, lotus-legged, on an altar, its eyes, made of pure jade, ablaze with a kind of diabolical fire. The mouth was pulled back to reveal wolf-like teeth in a fierce, hideous, and knowing grin. The great bulbous belly started at the fat, almost feminine breasts and protruded out some thirty feet over the knees. Two jagged horns on the forehead reached nearly to the ceiling, and, shockingly, on one was the impaled body of another fat mandarin, an obvious sacrifice.

"Ugly devil," Sir Roderick said in a low voice. "Hate to meet that in a dark alley."

"Look." Colin pointed to the necks of the mandarins. "They all seem to be wearing amulets of their god. Must have been some kind of insane cult. The worshippers are damned near as fat as he is. Gives me the willies."

"This chamber must be getting to me, Colin," said Sir Roderick. "I have the strangest feeling that the idol's eyes are watching me, following me around the room. Let's jolly well get the hell out of here."

"Wait." Colin yanked one of the amulets off a dead throat. "At least," he said, pitching it to Sir Roderick, "let's take a souvenir or two."

Sir Roderick looked at the jade figurine in his gloved palm, whose eyes bored into his own. "This little copy seems every bit as lethal as the original. Let's go." He tossed it back to Colin. "You keep it. Just touching it makes me feel, well, leprous."

Colin took another look at the figurine. Indeed, it did seem to send out a kind of snarling malevolence, but he shoved it into his pocket, gathered a few more yak waffles for chemical analysis back home, and they quit that awful place. Before they did, they took a last peek at the idol. Shuddered. Felt queasy.

Even in the blackness, without benefit of the flashlight on its face, the eyes shot out beams of feral madness.

On the Air India jet back to London, Sir Roderick maintained a highly untypical glumness, staring out at the cloudbanks, muttering things Colin could not decipher. But the latter's own foreboding was driven out by pretty hostesses serving drinks and by the thought that he had something in his possession that would guarantee a sensational TV special.

Then there was Camille standing at the gate of New York's Kennedy International as he deplaned, smothering him with her sweet, wispy kisses. "Well, darling, did you bring me back one of those enchanting sari dresses?"

"Sari, I didn't," Colin punned, back in comedic form at the sight of his willowy wife. "But I brought back something better. Here, I had it mounted on a chain."

And around that lovely neck he slipped the jade amulet.

Outside the terminal a wind from Canada whispered... *It's here... the horror is here...* to which a wind from the Bronx replied... *I know... I know... I know already...*

five

They decided to stay at the Plaza for a night of elegance, and fun on the town. Over cocktails at Manhattan's posh Four Seasons restaurant ("With the prices they're asking I think they want to pay it off in one season," Colin said), Camille brought him up to date on the Levittown gossip. The Hendersons had managed to get Little Red Riding Hood banned from the library on two counts: glorification of Communism and of organized crime. There'd been a savage shootout at the corner of Routes 13 and 1, with six dead, four wounded, and the gunman, as he was being carted off, was heard to say, "That's the last time I open my Exxon station on a Sunday."

Through the chitchat he noticed with mild surprise that Camille, whose appetite control center was always set at a firm, unshakable 350 calories per meal, had unwittingly polished off three orders of potatoes swimming in thick au gratin sauce, plus a forest of breadsticks. "Watch it, Camy," he chided, "another binge like that and you'll be up to a hundred and six pounds." At that she giggled; he'd caught her dipping her spoon into his French vanilla ice cream, and she put it down with a guilty smile.

They enjoyed the new Neil Simon production at the 46th Street theatre. The famed playwright had reworked Solzhenitsyn's *Gulag Archipelago,* with its theme of men being shipped to Stalinist slave labor camps in Siberia, into a hilarious two-act comedy entitled *Joe Sent Me.*

On the way to their room Camille stopped at the newsstand to buy a *Cosmopolitan* and somehow found her hand dropping a half-dozen Almond Joys into her large, Tijuana-manufactured purse. At the night table, now in a filmy shorty gown, she sprayed a dollop of Arpege on her earlobes and absentmindedly dug into the bag, munched a candy bar, and fondled the amulet around her neck. "Spooky little devil, isn't he? Got a name?"

"Name him whatever you want."

"Very well," and she held it up to the light. "'Cause you're such a fat little feller and you look like you have a hearty appetite and you look as round and jolly as Oliver Hardy, I dub thee," and those sweet lips kissed the belly of the figurine, "Captain Hardy."

There was a sudden swirling outside their window as a wind whipping over Central Park whispered to a wind coming up from the Bowery... *You see?... you see?... I told you I knew what I was talking about...*

"Camy, let's you and me and even Captain Hardy have a ménage à trois," he said with a lover's ferocity. "I haven't seen you in two weeks." He pulled her down on the bed, and it was all he had hoped for. Lips connecting, navels rubbing, legs intertwined, until she suggested by her eyes and movements that she desired to manipulate their bodies into the classical position of mutual oral sex. But with her ever-faulty comprehension of all things anatomical, as reflected in her art, she wound up paying lip service to his big toe until he guided her back to the far more acceptable sixty-nine configuration. After a panting five minutes during which all time and space was blocked out by their passion, they reached their climaxes.

Colin lay back, spent and content, but despite her orgasm something odd gleamed in Camille's eyes, her lips retracted, her teeth extruded, and without a warning she fell upon him like a starved lioness on the high veldt, biting and tearing until his pleasure changed to pain and he found himself sitting up and pushing her off. "Camy, I know you've missed me, but you've taken a chunk out of my thigh." True. There was a small, ugly hole there spurting blood. Snapping out of her dreamy state she plugged it with alcohol-soaked cotton and they fell asleep in each other's arms.

They made an early start and were back at 54 Dovedroppings by noon—and could have been back two hours sooner except that Camille had insisted on stopping at every Howard Johnson's on the Jersey Turnpike to visit the ladies room—she said. However, after each rest stop Colin detected the tang of mint, Milky Ways and Mr. Goodbars on her breath. She never mentioned buying the candy; he, although thinking it a bit strange, didn't push the matter. Louisiana, with a sumptuous lunch ready, greeted her "sweet chile." Locking Camille in a bear's embrace she said, "Honey, I wants you to try mah com fritters."

"Great, I'm starved!" Camille said, and picked a fat greasy one off the top of the pile before she even sat down. Colin as usual found some excuse to duck Louisiana's fare and settled for a modest asparagus salad which he prepared himself. Foster Hamilton then called at length to add more spice to the special, the news that Sammy Davis Jr. had been booked, would sing "Candy Man" while Colin created marzipan, taffy, and other confections, and would join in a finale exhibiting both his blackness and Jewishness, a recipe for matzohballs on collard greens.

"And we call it—now get this—Sol food, right?" Colin put in.

Hamilton bent over howling and dropped the phone.

During his chat with his father-in-law he was vaguely aware of a grunting noise throughout the house, and using his ten-foot telephone extension cord tracked it to the kitchen.

There he saw a sight that popped his eyes.

Camille. On her knees before the opened GE fridge. As though in prayer. Eyes scanning the interior. Hands curved like hawk talons, yanking out leftover spaghetti, pints of yogurt, and two large casaba melons. Without even resorting to silverware she jammed them into her mouth, even chomping down the thick melonskins, sounding more like the grinding of a garbage disposal than a human being.

"Cool it!" he shouted with annoyance. And she did, but not before she popped six black olives onto her tongue. "Still at it? You had ten fritters for lunch and half of my salad. Hey," and he grinned, "you're not... ?"

"No, darling. No little Carews on the way. Maybe it's those darn B-12 shots Mark gave me."

"Whatever it is, it's not too bad, me luv. Never seen you look quite so, uh, womanly. You must have put on five pounds since we met at the airport. What say to a flick tonight? That Brando thing is at the Eric."

"Oh, yes, *Last Mango in Paris*"

"That's *Tango*. I think you made a little Foodian slip, if you'll pardon the pun."

It might have been the intensity of the explicit sexual scenes that made Camille run several times to the popcorn stand. Certainly the moment when Brando lathered his penis with butter preparatory to sodomizing his paramour got to Camille, in a heavy way. This time she returned without the popcorn but with a huge cup of melted butter. "Oh," she said, while slurping it down, "I think I got a few drops on Captain Hardy." And she wiped the amulet clean.

Maybe she's just as nervous about this bigtime TV thing as I am, Colin thought. That could account for all the nibbling.

Again he ignored it.

But later that night things took a sharp turn.

To begin with she suggested they forsake the usual Johnny Carson show. "Tonight I think I'd rather watch Dick Cabbage—uh—Cavett."

He gave her a hard look. The second slip in one day. That, coupled with the pound of Brazil nuts she ate during the telecast, started a nagging worry in his mind. At 1 A.M. she still had no desire to call it a night, looking through the *TV Guide* for a late movie. "Ooooh, Channel Three, Lon Chaney Jr. in *The Vampire Returns*" And he assented to watching, happy that for the nonce the idea of food had left her.

"Gee," she said about 2:30 A.M. "Here's the big scene where Dr. Van Helsing tracks him to the coffin and drives a stake through his—" Suddenly that enigmatic fervor had contorted her face again. "—Oh, God, steak, *steak!*" She leaped from their canopied bed and dashed into the hallway. Shaken, Colin took after her, and when the kitchen light flared he saw Camille.

Down on her knees again. Tongue flicking out obscenely like a Linda Lovelace. Deep-throating a gigantic T-bone steak. Gurgling. Crooning. Sighing.

"Camy!" He knocked the glistening white bone, completely devoid of meat, from her mouth. "For God's sake stop it and come to bed."

They lay in the darkness, silent, as though there was an unspoken agreement not to bring up the kinky scene that had just occurred in the kitchen. It's over, he thought, and turned to catch what was left of a night's sleep. There was a stirring on her side of the bed. A tiny hand sliding down his chest. Making the hair on his navel flutter. Then loosening the cord to his p.j. bottoms. Her hair fell like a wave over his belly; her lips found what they were seeking. *Good Lord,* he thought, shaking, albeit in pleasure.

She's eating again.

six

With the cheery notes of a mockingbird (who was operating in the wrong section of Levittown; by ordinance he should have been trilling his wakeup melodies in his own part of town, Mockingbirdmerde Road), Colin got up, sleepily recalled the outlandishness of his wife's nocturnal behavior, shaved, showered, all the while hoping she was just being seized by a passing caprice. Swabbing on a last dash of English Leather, rejoicing in the bracing sting it always gave his good looks, he stepped on the large, highly accurate doctor's scale next to the clothes hamper. Weighing himself was a highly necessary morning ritual to insure that though he was in the food game he would retain his constant, attractive 165-pound level. There was no excuse for looking like a beefy slob on TV. This same weigh-in was also part of Camille's getting-up ritual, and obviously she had been there first. He blinked when he saw the setting.

One hundred nineteen pounds.

Good Lord, she had kissed her 105-pound weight goodbye with a fury. Fourteen pounds in two days! Unless the scale was on the fritz.

But when he readjusted it and obtained his familiar, pleasing 165 he knew his fear was not groundless.

Slipping on orange slacks and a fawn-colored pullover, he sauntered into the kitchen. Louisiana, mop in hand, turned to say, "Lawd A-mighty, Missuh Colin, dat sweet chile o' yours done whupped a load of mah buckwheat cakes upside de head. I never seen such eatin' in all mah born days. I do believe somethin' done got into dat sweet chile. I gonna look in mah voodoo dream book and see if ah can see sumpin' that has a possible manifestation of some inner emotional turmoil which translates itself into..." She stopped quickly. I'd better go back to the do-rag bit, she thought, or I'll blow this cushy gig and wind up back in New Orleans working my self sick as the regional director for Operation Breadbasket.

With a "Yuck, yuck, yuck," she shuffled off, humming a spiritual.

But Colin, with so much to do of his own, let that slide as well, and dug in for the day's work. He sketched out show ideas, wrofe a few more food parodies *(When the hell are they going to invent a word that rhymes with orange?)*, called Levi Flare about a big midshow Mount Everest number (the girls in yak suits, the boys as Dalai Lamas), and found himself famished by five o'clock; but since they were to attend a party at the Hendersons later that evening he contented himself with a slice of Melba toast and a wedge of cheddar cheese. To check on Camille, he rang up the boutique and was informed by her salesgirl, Toni, that she hadn't been there for most of the day. "Oh Colin, she ducked out for an early lunch and just never got back."

He heard the crunch of her Fiat 850 tires in the driveway, then the crunch of her heels on the gravel walk and then another crunch, this one a long, crashing CR-R-R-RUNNNNNNNCHHHHHHH! He ran to the kitchen window to see Camille taking a stupendous bite out of an extra-crispy Colonel Sanders chicken thigh, her eyes lit by that strange glow, a greasy finger fondling Captain Hardy and then, guiltily stuffing the great wax bucket, which surely must have held at least twenty-one pieces of the old Kentuckian's finger-lickin' fowl, deep into the garbage can.

She entered and offered her lips, generally so sweet lead her natural essence. Now it was like kissing a lube rack. "Colin," she sighed, "what time is the party? I haven't had a morsel all day."

He bit his lip. Stifled an urge to scream, *Liar, liar!* Put a bogus smile on his face. Let her into the living room and watched her left hand work slyly into the ashtray and pull out the last crumbs of cheese and Melba toast he'd left.

The right one fondled the jade figurine.

"Oh darn!" She was putting on her party clothes now and she let go her strongest epithet in front of the blue-tinged full-length mirror on the door of their walk-in closet. "I've gotta say something to those cleaners. They've shrunk my nicest skirt."

And outside the wind, knowing what had been promised as coming, what was coming, and when it would come, whispered... *the skirt, the skirt... the horror has started with the skirt...*

seven

Hank and Helen annually threw a glittering soiree to mark William F. Buckley's birthday, and as usual Levittown's elite had parked their Jags and Porsches all over Dovedroppings Lane and were marching to the back patio festooned with Chinese lanterns (Taiwanese, not mainland) where the festivities were in full swing. Cohn and Camille walked in to find the liberal Rosenblatts and the rightist Hendersons jawing away about politics, the argument vigorous but not unfriendly. The banker had the mattress designer by the lapels of his double-knit jacket and was hammering home his point. "Arnold, I think the US should not only get out of the UN, but out of the Western Hemisphere. The whole place is honeycombed with leftist elements."

"Where would you go, Hank?" Rosenblatt smiled.

"Australia. Move in lock, stock, and barrel."

A round of kissing, caressing and backslapping greeted the Carews; Colin, as the resident celebrity was much admired and envied by all. He pushed through several flirtatious housewives to get to Dr. Mark Twine, their family GP, who rarely had to administer to this basically lean and healthy couple. Camille eyed a waitress tiptoeing across the lawn with a tray of Swedish meatballs and cocktail franks and followed her until it was thoroughly cleaned out.

"Mark," Colin pulled the doctor to him confidentially. "I wish you'd take a look at Camille. She's undergone a funny change and developed a fantastic appetite."

Dr. Twine glanced at Camille, now like an Algonquin warrior on the trail of another canapé-carrying waitress, her long fingernails stabbing out frequently to spear an artichoke right in the heart and draw it back to her glistening mouth.

"Healthy appetite I'd say, Colin, but nothing to concern yourself about. She's a trifle more zoftig than usual, but you can't expect her to look like Mia Farrow forever. If she runs into any problems, give me a buzz and we'll check it out."

And Dr. Twine turned to meet a confrere and a newcomer to the community. He was bearded and goateed Dr. Sigmund Kawpdrayer, the outstanding psychiatrist, whose office on Swallowspoor Lane was a haven for housewives seeking an end to frigidity and husbands seeking a resumption of rigidity. The two professionals exchanged handclasps and launched into a meaningful discussion on fee-splitting. Dr. Twine, remembering his social graces, said, "Oh, Siggy, this is my good friend, Cohn Carew."

"Ah, the Giggling Gourmet, you of the recipes and the clever songs. You are truly a favorite in my household. Now," and he sent a teasing look of challenge, "could you create on the spot a song parody about a headshrinker?"

The crowd which gathered about Colin stopped its mundane chatter about Nicklaus backswings and Billie Jean forehands, stilled, waiting to see if Colin could pass this test of wit.

Colin flipped through the Rolodex of his mind, let free association have its way, and to a Sinatra standard sang:

> *"Scary tales from a grouch,*
> *Can be cured on a couch,*
> *If you're Jung at heart.*
> *Even Adler and Freud,*
> *Never could be annoyed,*

If you're Jung at heart!"

There was a spontaneous burst of laughter and applause and Dr. Kawpdrayer thundered, "Capital! Jung at heart. I must use that one at our next convention." The tension released by Colin's mirth, the guests swarmed to the buffet table and began piling on the turkey legs, cold cuts, avocado salads, and Jell-o molds topped with sour cream. Camille was the very first in line, only taking a bit of this and that, but in a quiet way heaping enough on her plate to feed an underdeveloped nation. Then someone started the latest dirty joke, "Did you hear the one about the pervert and the pelican? The pervert sees this pelican on the beach... and you know what pelicans do..."

A fast elbow in the ribs from his wife stopped him just in time, because at that moment three august men, the representatives of Levittown's Inter-Faith Council, walked into the party. There was Father Damien Blatty, slender, fortyish, a shock of dark hair falling over two burning eyes that had seen a million transgressions—perhaps two million, for sin like everything else was rising in this inflationary spiral. Father Blatty, a Jesuit from Georgetown, was the spiritual leader of Our Lady of the Rafflebook, the area's leading Roman Catholic church. He wore his traditional black suit and priest's collar. Next was the tall, patrician Dr. Romilar Desmond, the minister of St. Joseph of the Aspirin Episcopal Church, in his grey business suit and regimental tie. Trailing behind came the chubby Rabbi Zalman Bindlebinder of Temple Bet Midler, the leading synagogue. The trio had worked together for many months on projects involving the area's disadvantaged, and despite their theological differences, they held one another in mutual esteem.

The party waxed on. More food was consumed, more wine bottles uncorked, and Colin spotted Camille back in the buffet line for seconds—or was it thirds? He was so busy chatting with his many fans that he hadn't kept exact count.

"*Attendez-vous,* everybody!" It was Helen Henderson sounding a clarion call. "Cake time!" And there was a buzz of excitement. Helen's cakes, all homemade, were always masterpieces of icing and filling. Camille's eyes blinked and she touched Captain Hardy at the sight of two huge cakes being wheeled out by the waitresses.

"Okay, let's put the angel's food cake on the right, 'cause all us conservatives are angels," she said, and the throng chuckled. "The other one goes on the left. You liberals know what sinners you are."

The two cakes stood side by side, the angel food with its fleecy whiteness looking like a great halo, pure, chaste, and innocent. The other, a devil's food cake, was sinister in its rich brownness, the face of old Scratch that Helen had squeezed on its top with orange icing alive with menace.

"Well, who's first?" Helen said.

The sight of these two tantalizing structures intrigued all present, but they hesitated, making mental computations on the numbers of calories they'd already packed in. For a second no one moved.

There was a nervous laugh from Helen. "Here's our first customer."

It was Camille.

She moved forward. Slowly. As though in a trance. Driven by something.

She stood between the two cakes, uncertain of her choice. Gazed into their creamy lushness. Her tongue making small circles around her lips. Everybody hushed. Colin leaning forward. Dr. Twine taking a clinical look. Dr. Kawpdrayer tugging at his foxy beard.

"Come on, Camille," Helen nudged. "Angel's food or devil's food?"

Camille's hand flew to the amulet, gripped it. She shrieked, "The hell with heaven... I'm going straight to the fucking devil!"

A gasp came out of the crowd at her incredible invective, and then another when she hoisted the angel's food cake and hurled it squarely into Helen's face. Helen fell back, blinded by soggy drippings that began rolling down her cheeks, a choking sound in her cake-filled mouth.

With another blood-chilling scream Camille, though tiny in stature, lifted the fifteen-pound devil's food cake above her head, as though offering it to a dark deity. "I obey, I obey!" And brought it down again to her mouth and began tearing huge brown chunks out of it, slurping and sucking it down, quivering and falling forward on her chocolate-smeared face in a dead faint.

Colin, staggering and held up by Dr. Twine, was near to fainting himself from horror. The Giggling Gourmet knew one thing if he knew anything. That rasping scream that had rumbled out of his wife's mouth was not the voice of Camille Carew.

And the winds began to howl and whisper to each other... *See, first the too-tight skirt... now the shtick with the cake... did I tell you horror was coming or didn't I?...*

II: The Middle

Don't quote me.

BARTLETT

one

        Camille slept soundly, her hand still clutching Captain Hardy, whose wicked grin seemed to have widened a trifle. Or were Colin's glazed eyes sending illusions to his brain? He had put her to bed still in the cake-smeared outfit, the skirt split completely at the seams. Dr. Twine had diagnosed it as a simple swoon due to excitement or a drop too much wine, a common-enough occurrence at a party, but added, "If she acts up later, bring her over for an exam."

    Colin's apologies had been received in good grace by the Hendersons, but the shocked party had broken up quickly and news of her bizarre behavior was bound to permeate the community. He would face that as best he could.

    "Mah sweet chile sho' done had a bad night," Louisiana clucked, handing him the phone. "It's long distance, Missuh Colin." He went into the kitchen.

    It was Hubert Orkney on the other end from London. Collect. Which meant his balloon-squeezing act wasn't setting the world on fire.

    "Bad news, Alfie boy. I mean, Colin. It's Mum."

    "Mum? Mum?"

    "I'm afraid old Mum is gone. We were at a football match, sitting way up in the cheap seats. Things haven't been going too well financially, you know. When East Shoreditch kicked off against West Twickham, old Mum got so excited she jumped up and leaned forward to cheer the lads. That was her undoing, my boy. Those great breasts, like cargo shifting in the hold of an old tramp steamer, not to say that Mum was an old tramp, y' know... well, they broke out of her bra, swung over the railing, and pulled her out of the stands. She fell two hundred fifty feet."

"Good Lord," Colin said. "I'll come for the funeral immediately."

"No need to, Colin. You can't bury something you can't find. Alas, poor old Mum made such a hole when she went down that she landed on an unexploded German bomb buried under the playing field since 1944. It went off. Luckily no one else was hurt. The teams observed a moment of silence in her honor, continued playing around the crater, and finished the game."

"Who won?" Colin, ever the keen soccer buff, could not resist the query.

"Oh, West Twickham, three to two."

"Splendid. Did Derek Dalby do well?"

"Yes, kicked the winning goal, as a matter of fact."

"Good show! And what about the new center forward they got in trade from South Swappingham?"

"You mean Nicholas Nickleby?"

"Yes, that's the chap, Nicholas Nickleby."

"Played like the Dickens."

"Oh, ripping, ripping! Well, good-bye, Hubert, and thanks for calling." Colin hung up.

Then the shock set in. West Twickham had won? How odd! They hadn't bested East Shoreditch in years. And then the guilt set in. Why think about football when Mum was gone, when there was so much he should have said to her, when he should have invited her to enjoy his home, his bride and his celebrity? Now it was too late. And he buried his head in his hands.

He was suddenly conscious of the fact that Camille was entering on a ghostly tread into the kitchen. "Darling," he sobbed. "Mum's dead."

"What's for lunch?" she snarled. "Stop fucking around and give me some food. You're the great Giggling Gourmet, so shove something soft and creamy between my teeth and make it snappy. I can't wait all fucking day."

Stunned, he stood there.

"All right," she sneered. Her voice, usually so high-pitched and silvery, had begun to thicken. "I'll help myself." She lunged at the cupboard, pulled out a box of Mallomars, and bit savagely right through the cardboard, her teeth crushing the plump chocolate-covered marshmallow crackers, her tongue hissing python-like as it licked at the spongy filling.

"Stop it, Camy. You're acting irrational again." "Devil's food cake. I want *more* devil's food cake." "You know we don't have any in the house."

"Then I'll take," and her eyes rolled madly, "these." She grabbed at a Saran-wrapped bowl on the kitchen table. "Deviled eggs, Colin, deviled eggs!" And she began cooing and cackling as her tongue licked out the mustard and mayonnaise from the hollowed-out hard-boiled egg whites. "Deviled eggs, Colin, made with," and she laughed hideously, "Hellmann's mayonnaise. *Hell*-mann's. Fuck Miracle Whip. It's *Hell*mann's my body wants. *Hell, hell, hell... !*"

She ran screaming from the kitchen, bumped squarely into the entering Lousiana, and cried out, "Ah, you big chocolate baby. I'd like to eat all two hundred fifty pounds of you!" She bit Louisiana's arm, laughed harshly again, and ran into the bathroom.

Colin whispered to the trembling maid. "She's gone bananas."

"Bananas?" It was Camille, charging back into the kitchen. "I heard that. Where? Where are the bananas?" She ran to a fruitbowl on the table and grasped a bunch of bananas, said, "Look, Captain Hardy!" to the amulet, "bananas!" Tucking the bunch under her arm she ran off, singing, "Day-o, day-o, daylight come and me wanna go home..."

Colin, his head spinning, his stomach queasy, went to the bathroom, extracted a large bottle of Pepto Bismol from the cabinet, and drained half of it down. There, that was better. He leaned against the sink, feeling the waves of nausea subside. Then his eye caught the bathroom scale...

It was at 134.

My God, she'd put on another huge block of blub. But why?

He called Dr. Twine and made an appointment for the following day.

two

Camille spent a restful night, not once arising to raid the fridge. On the morrow she seemed more like her old self, but Louisiana kept a suspicious watch on her "sweet chile."

On the way to Dr. Twine's she did insist they stop for a malted at a local sweet shop. Colin permitted the indulgence, happy that she had agreed to the appointment and hoping it would turn the situation around.

He sat in the outer office leafing idly through a battered magazine filled with stories about millions of people out of work and on welfare lines, forced to burn wood in their homes, reading by candlelight, thinking to himself, "A typical doctor's office. Magazines forty years old," until he saw on the back cover an ad for the 1974 Vega and realized it was the current issue of *Time*.

Two hours later Dr. Twine called him in for a consultation. A subdued Camille sat, her hands folded demurely, a wispy, guilty smile on her face.

"Colin, I've made a few tests, all negative, but in view of her weight gain I think we ought to check to see whether it's exogenous obesity, which means she's ingesting more than the body can burn off, or endogenous obesity, which often has a glandular source. We'll run off some more tests, a T-3, a PBI, an NYU—scratch that last one, that's my alma mater. We should send her to the hospital for those tests and also a serum amylase and serum trypasin, upper and lower GI, gall bladder, brain scan, anything that could possibly have a bearing on systemic malfunction."

Colin said, "That's okay. Sooner the better." And Camille nodded her assent.

She was hospitalized for three days.

The results: negative. No systemic malfunction.

But she gained three pounds.

"Three more pounds?" Colin snapped at Dr. Twine when he brought her back to the medico's office for a followup conference.

"The nurse told me she developed a fondness for swallowing strawberry-flavored barium, ten bottles a day. Camille, it's a nine-hundred-calorie-a-day diet for you, and in a few weeks I want to see that fat come off."

"Uh," said Camille, going into dietetic plea-bargaining, "couldn't you make it twelve hundred calories a day?"

Dr. Twine laughed, "OK, one thousand, but that's my last offer."

For the next few days Louisiana was weighing out the portions like a gold dealer on the London exchange—two ounces of this, three ounces of that, grapefruit sections, kale, Blue Lake string beans—and Camille dutifully ate whatever she was given, never once balking, never once seen going to the GE for noshing.

A week later Colin put her on the scale.

She had gained ten pounds.

Impossible! Either he or Louisiana had monitored every meal.

"I don't understand it, Colin. Must be something the doctor missed." With a shrug of unconcern, she said, "I'm going to the rec room and work on my Thor."

"OK, you do that. I'm going into Philly to interview some choreographers and writers. Now mind yourself and be a good little—" He looked at her size—"well, a good girl. Remember, only celery for midday nourishment."

"Yes, darling," she said sweetly. "Only celery." And began slapping handfuls of clay onto the statue. When he left, she called out, "Louisiana, can I have a snack please?" Then remembered. Louisiana had taken the day off to attend the New York wedding of two old friends, Uncle Ben and Aunt Jemima, where the invited guests would throw rice and pancakes at the happy couple. A smile gathered at the corners of Camille's mouth. She was alone.

She put down the clay, wiped her hands on her smock, and had a quick need to touch Captain Hardy. Then she went into the kitchen and opened the fridge. Frowned. Nothing but celery stalks stacked like cordwood. That damn Colin! He'd tried to keep all temptation from her. *But I'm smarter than he thinks.*

From a drawer she took a large breadknife.

Two blocks from the house Colin remembered. He'd left his list of show ideas on the desk in the den. He turned the Mercedes around and headed back to Dovedroppings Lane. Parked. Walked up the driveway. Took out his housekey.

There was Camille in the living room. Standing on a chair, knife in hand, stabbing with a fierce grunt of effort into something in the crystal chandelier. There was a soft squoosh and she pulled out the knife, an impaled Sara Lee cheesecake halfway up the blade. Began sinking her teeth into it, growling and snapping, then releasing deep sighs of fulfillment.

"Camille!"

She wheeled, eyes ablaze with hate. "You fucking snooper, you dirty son of a bitch of a sneak!" Again her voice had that new thickened and ugly tone that caused the cords of her neck to bulge out like tortured ropes.

"Give me that cake and that knife."

"The cake I keep," and she finished it with one long swallow. "The knife is for you, my dear husband."

She leaped off the chair, the knife glinting in her hand, and swung it toward his chest. He ducked and she flew by, tripped and fell into the couch, the blade scoring a great slash into the velvet covering.

Out tumbled thousands and thousands of little multi-colored tablets, which she began to shove into her mouth at an incredible rate. "Oh, so good, so good..." she moaned, as though having a sexual climax.

He kneeled, picked up a handful of the tablets. "My God, the whole couch is stuffed with M&Ms!" In the heat of his anger they melted in his hands, not his mouth.

He pulled her up and slapped her face. She came out of her wolfish state. "All right, damn you, where's the rest of it? I know there's more."

"Please, Colin, please..."

He slapped her again. "Show me, you little devil." Outside one wind whispered to another... *He knows... he knows... he's no dummy...*

"All right." She led him through the house, unearthing all her little hidden caches of forbidden fruit. The first was literally that, a spring bonnet among her hat collection that was adorned with real cherries and strawberries, not plastic ones. The sampler she had been stitching was a veritable Whitman Sampler and quite edible, the black and red strings pure licorice. The fishbowl: its marbles buried in the sand were not agates or alleys, but Charms sourballs. (The fish, he knew, had been consumed long ago.) And the crystalline wind chimes that tinkled in each breeze—old-fashioned rock candy on strings. "My God," he said. "Why stop there? Why not eat the kitchen sink?" And had a sudden thought. Ran to it. Felt it. Thank heaven, still porcelain. But he clumsily knocked over a can of new Comet, Josephine the Plumber's brand. It poured down on a stain near the sink's drain, but unlike the TV commercial did not bleach it out. Why? On a hunch he put a finger in the spilled substance and brought it to his lips. No cleanser. *Pure sugar!*

He gave her a ten-milligram Valium and soon she was dozing, the hardness off her face, the sweet cherubic look back.

"Mark," he said anxiously into the phone, "how can you say those tests were negative? She's eating like there was no tomorrow. I've been rummaging through some of the household bills. You know how much bread she's been eating? Russia didn't steal that much wheat from us. And the milk lobby should move into my house, not Washington."

"Colin, we made exhaustive tests. There's nothing physical. Tell you what. Why don't you enroll her in the Fat Fighters? I understand they're doing wonders. Maybe with a little moral support she can lick this thing."

three

Two dozen ladies, each with one hand pressed over the heart, the other over the stomach, stood facing a life-sized likeness of Marianna Trench, the founder of the newest of the diet-cum-confessional weight-reducing organizations, Fat Fighters. The cardboard statuette depicted a woman who was tall and tan and young and lovely—and, incidentally, living in a luxurious hotel in Ipanema, which she owned, only part of her multi-million-dollar fortune derived from the four-hundred-chapter organization she had built over two years.

In unison they said, "I pledge allegiance to Fat Fighters of America and to the principles for which it stands, one organization under God, and underweight... dedicated to making our fat invisible... with skinniness and size-eight dresses for all."

They sat down in the meeting room of the local Moose Hall lodge, Camille's chair creaking under her 190-pound load. Colin, who had dropped her off, decided to wait in the parking lot. It would not do for a man known as the Giggling Gourmet, the purveyor of rich foods, to enter this citadel of self-control, lest he reignite an urge each had been stoutly battling.

A woman walked to the podium. "I am your president, Mrs. Geraldine Potter of 13 Spewingswine Lane, and I am a foodaholic. Two months ago I weighed 210 pounds. To conceal my size I wore shapeless muu-muu dresses by day and for parties at night a basic black barrel, maybe with a single strand of pearls. Sex was gone from my life. The only time my hubby touched me was to put his feet up on me. He thought I was a hassock. When I jumped into our backyard swimming pool, the splash was like Old Faithful spurting up in Yellowstone Park. I was bored, lonely, unhappy, and lost myself in cupcakes and candy. Then I heard about Fat Fighters. I put my hand into Marianna Trench's, and felt the healing waves of her philosophy wash over me. I started on her Number Nine diet—"

"Amen, sister!" the others called out.

"—the diet with the hot Indian powder topped with spinach leaves. The curry with the fringe on top—"

"Hallelujah, Sister Potter. Hallelujah!"

"I fought my battle with fat and won, but not alone. With all of my sisters here, who when I felt like slipping back would rush over and force Fresca down my throat."

"Blessed be the name of Fresca, for it has made us free!" they cried.

"And I have learned," she went on, "how to make the most tasty treats out of low-calorie foods. Delicious Danish pastries out of asparagus tips and beet root. Marvelous and filling milk shakes with a pinch of nonfat milk, a packet of Sweet'N Low and just a gallon and a half of water. Now I am down to a hundred and thirty pounds and still in there dieting. It has become a way of life. Sex is back—not with my husband, that fat slob, but with the handsome dog of a delivery boy who brings the spinach, the asparagus, and the nonfat milk."

"All praise to Fat Fighters!" the chorus echoed. "We shall never again be tempted by fatty foods. Our spirit will sustain us!"

Mrs. Potter smilingly pointed to Camille. "We have a new member with us tonight, a lovely young woman you know from her art boutique and the many community-minded things she has done. She has come to us in her hour of need and we will show her the light. Tell us your story, Mrs. Camille Carew."

Camille puffed her way to the podium and looked at a sea of shining faces.

"Oh, my sisters, as you can see I have been a naughty girl. Only a short time ago I weighed a hundred and five pounds. Now I am nearing two hundred."

There was a plaintive ahhhh from the crowd. "We'll help you, Sister Carew!" cried a woman.

"And why have I swollen to this size? Because of this!" She opened her handbag, producing a large jelly doughnut. There were gasps of "Terrible, terrible!" Camille squeezed it; a rivulet of grape jelly burst out and rolled down its greasy side, which she licked.

"This did it to me... and this—" Now she fished out a brick of Swiss chocolate and nibbled off a corner. "Remember these awful temptations, how they felt when they slid into your stomach?"

"Oh my God," a front-row member said, clenching her fist.

"And this—" she pulled out a poundcake, "and this—" an eclair, "and this—" a Charlotte Russe, placing them all upon the podium. The women stirred nervously, squeezing their eyes shut, popping Trident gum into their twitching mouths.

"And this, my dears—" Suddenly there was a malicious slyness in her voice. She pulled out a dozen Stauffer's Devil Fudge cupcakes. "Here!" She flung them into the crowd, who by now had abandoned their restraint and rushed forward like a pack of maddened dingo dogs. "Here, the devil's delight. My master's gift..

Mrs. Potter said, "Girls, no! Remember Marianna Trench..."

"Fuck Marianna Trench!" Camille screamed with fiendish glee. "Eat, eat, eat!"

And touched Captain Hardy again.

The food she had brought disappeared in ten seconds. When it was gone, she cried, "Come, follow me! On to Howard Johnson's!" And they did, crashing out of the Moose Lodge into the night, a parade of starved, screaming banshees. Mrs. Potter said to herself, "What the hell?" picked herself up, yanked the moosehead down from the wall, took a bite out of it, and joined the rampaging group now streaming across the street into that orange and green home of datenut bread and fried Ipswich clams and baked beans. The orgy had begun.

Colin, watching Camille lead the ravenous pack, slumped into the Mercedes and prayed.

And the ever-watching winds whispered among themselves... *Oh, boy, the horror is having a ball tonight!*

four

The days passed. Horribly. Revoltingly.

There was very little conversation between Colin and Camille. And when there was, there were more of those slips of the tongue and mind that furthered his belief that she was in thrall to a terrible food fixation. She had a desire to watch suave, black-suited Duncan Renaldo on Channel Six in a grainy old Western, *The Crisco Kid.*

"That's *Cisco*," he said, irritated.

"On second thought I'd rather see Dick Van Duck."

"Dyke." His anger was rising.

"Give me that fucking *TV Guide*," she demanded, yanking the magazine from his hand, the obscenity again making him cringe. "Let me see," and her tongue undulated out in serpent-like fashion. "Ah, here. Something that really turns me on."

He looked at the screen. This show? For which in the past she had expressed a positive loathing? But he knew why. It was *The Partridge Family.* And she was lapping it up, it and the large bag of Wise potato chips on her lap, which had begun to disappear with the spreading girth.

And she found more and more time to watch the set because that gave her excuses to eat more and more TV dinners. Soon even that phase worsened. One day he caught her on the couch eating a TV dinner. And the set was off. And the dinner was still frozen.

On another day he came into her rec room studio. She was working again and he felt pleased for a moment. Then he looked at her labors and a soundless scream tugged out of his soul.

She had finished her great god, Thor, and was leaning back to inspect it. The top half of the body was as before, muscular and magnificent, anatomically correct except for the minor flaw of a third eye in the chin, which he dismissed.

But the bottom... oh, Jesus, the bottom! Where the genitals should have been—a long zucchini squash for a penis, flanked by two large Jersey beefsteak tomatoes as testes.

"Stop it, stop it!" Now his scream was audible. She had fallen to her knees and was eating the sexual salad, more hideous noises scratching out of her throat.

On another day an anxious-faced Rona met him in the driveway. "Colin, have you seen Sihanouk? He's been missing for a couple of days and Arnold and I are worried. Maybe he sneaked into your house."

"Why not ask Camille?"

"Oh, Colin, I couldn't. I can't stand to face her anymore. She looks so..." Rona scurried to her own door, sobbing bitterly.

Colin walked into the bedroom. There was Camille, sitting up, her cheeks puffed out like tennis balls, her body covering most of their canopied double bed (which he had long since vacated in favor of a couch in his den, so unappealing a bed partner was she). Wearing a grin of mockery.

"Have you seen that Siamese cat of Rona's?"

"Why ask me, my dear husband?" It was the voice of a hag. "What the fuck do I care about a goddam cat?" But when she began laughing diabolically, he shook her shoulders, knowing she was lying. Because large hairballs were floating out of her lips and around the room.

"Where is Sihanouk?" he shouted.

She said, "I have no idea." But two claws were regurgitated out, followed by a velvet collar with a little bell.

"You ate him, oh Jesus, you ate him..."

She smiled a great smile. And began to sing in an Oriental accent, "I am Siamese if you please... I am Siamese if you don't please..." and gave one of Sihanouk's silky and sassy meows.

He could stand it no longer. Rushed to the bathroom to chuck up. Bent over the sink. Gagged, then let go...

But there was a hand tickling his buttocks.

He turned.

It was Camille, her eyes brilliant with hellfire.

"See, Colin, see." And she panted and stepped on the doctor's scale. Shoved the brass weights to the furthest position on the right.

There was a crack like a low-yield nuclear bomb. The bathroom shook. He heard the scream of tortured metal and saw the scale crumble.

She had reached the three-hundred-pound level. And smashed it.

five

In the rays of the setting sun the last few bathers on Santa Monica beach were gathering up their blankets and Thermos bottles and their portable radios, those umbilical links to the world outside, and starting up the paths to their autos. The craggy man on the beach finished his two-thousandth deep knee-bend, rewarded himself for the exertion with a bite of the original organic food, lava, a chunk of which he kept always in his pocket. A trifle hard on the teeth, perhaps, but loaded with nourishing minerals of all kinds—iron, nickel, copper. True, he clanked sometimes when he walked, and on his yearly physical his doctor had prescribed drinking two tablespoons of Rustoleum each day, but it was worth it to Romaine LeLane, The Exerciser.

"Hey, mister." A little boy of perhaps three tugged at his massive arm. "Could you please help me find my beachball? It's over there somewhere." He indicated a section still populated by a few remaining sun worshippers.

"Of course, my child," LeLane said in his sonorous voice. He proceeded to the spot, arriving there by dint of ten cartwheels (why waste an opportunity to tumble?), and saw a round object with red stripes upon it. He bent to retrieve it, and a man got up roaring, "Take your damn hands off my stomach! What are you, some kind of a fag?"

Good Lord, LeLane thought. That round ball *is* a stomach, the red stripes streaks of sunburn! How could a young man—and the bearer of this Buddha-like belly surely could not have been more than forty—let himself go like this, that great ball of fat hanging over his bathing trunks? Now he looked at the others... all of them, men and women, had spare-tire stomachs, arms dripping with flab, pouches under the eyes.

And why not? Their lunchboxes were filled with Hydrox cookies, greasy pastrami, white bread made of library paste, all supplied by the giant food chains, those cathedrals of obesity, bulging with every imaginable kind of fatty food. Was it any wonder the world was going to hell in a market basket? And that he had been canceled in favor of a clever young man who knew just how to exploit this insane rush for calories?

Was there any more use for a man who believed in the virtues of a lean, bemuscled body? It seemed not. Where could an old muscleman go? What could he do to combat this terrible thing that was turning his countrymen into mounds of soft, buttery pulp?

But the wind whispered to him... *take heart, old lion... you will yet be needed for the fight of your life...*

And as though he had heard its warning, he began to gird himself for the struggle, squeezing the medicine out of his medicine ball, flexing and punishing his muscles beyond the breaking point, and then lifting the lifeguard's dory high over his head like a barbell.

"Put the damn boat down," a voice cried. "Can't you see I'm humping a chick under the tarpaulin?"

And the wind whispered... *they're coming... they're coming...*

It was a week later. Colin sat at the supper table, picking listlessly at Louisiana's collard greens, his father-in-law seated across from him.

"Have you heard from Camille, son?"

"I called this afternoon. They said things are going along okay."

"Can they really do her any good?"

Colin's fork toyed with a black-eyed pea. "Listen, dad, the Last Chance Health Farm is the nth-degree in reducing resorts. That Arizona ranch has everything—saunas, massages, round-the-clock treatment, supervised diets, doctors, health experts, mud baths, the works. If the wealthiest socialites in the world go there, maybe there's a chance for Camille. Listen, about the show—"

"Don't worry about the show. Levi Flare's taking over things. He'll have it whipped into good shape. You just concentrate on Camille. But I hope to God it isn't one of those health farms that's right across the street from a Pizza Hut. You know, they starve all day and sneak out at night to load up."

"The Last Chance is right in the middle of the Painted Desert, fifty miles from the nearest town. They have barbed wire fences, guard dogs. Papillon couldn't get her out."

Hamilton looked at his watch. "Gotta go. I'll call you tomorrow."

Watching Hamilton's limousine jet away, he realized he was now alone. Of course, there was Louisiana, but she was upstairs watching the Dean Martin roast of Anwar Sadat. Of late even the trusty maid had begun to act oddly, with strange noises and chants coming out of the second-story bedroom. Some bayou nonsense, he supposed.

He went into the rec room and spotted one of his wife's unfinished paintings; despite his gully-low misery laughed aloud. Camy's version of Whistler's Mother had the old woman out of the chair and on her knees, definitely off her rocker. She'd done it again. How he missed her, the way she used to be before this revolting transmutation. Now all Levittown knew about the Hendersons' party and the debacle at the Fat Fighters meeting, and they'd begun peering into the boutique window, watching her gobble loaf after loaf of raisin bread, pointing and whispering. When she'd reached 305 pounds he'd had no choice but to ship her to the resort.

The Rosenblatts stopped over around ten-thirty, Rona with a card from Camille. "She says she's having a wonderful time, Colin. Thank God, they're doing something for her out there. I just know it'll work out. We all miss her." Then Arnold said, "Hey lover, we've got a new mattress to test tonight. Let's get to the launch pad." And they left.

Well, he thought, over a bedside cup of tea, she'll be back in a month.

As it turned out, she was back the next morning—in a Brinks truck which pulled into the driveway. The driver, a man whose haggard face looked as though he had seen Dante's Inferno from an expensive pit-side seat, said tersely, "Sign this, buddy, and let me get the hell out of here."

From the back of the armored, sealed vehicle came an angry croak. "Let me go, you motherfucker. Let me out of here or I'll smash this truck to bits." A shattering blow landed on a side wall of the vehicle, the force causing the front headlights to fall off.

The driver blanched. "It's a damn good thing they injected her with massive doses of Thorazine before we left Arizona. That kept her pretty well knocked out for the first three days, but yesterday she began to come out of it and started banging the walls. Look at the truck!" He pointed to scores of bulges on its exterior, imprints of knuckles in the iron. "Go on sign, and let me go," he begged.

Colin signed. The driver unlocked the back and ducked into the cab.

Camille blinked at the rays of the sun. "So..." Her voice was again the sinister one of the witch hag in Snow White. "So... I'm back to my dear spouse. Dig my body, lover?"

The face was bloated almost beyond recognition—the eyes had become sunken in the swollen face, though they flashed a baleful fire; the lips, those sweet lips he had so often kissed, now looked like two doughnuts back to back. "Feed me, honey, or I'll tear this fucking neighborhood apart."

He led her into the house and in desperation threw open the door of the GE. "Eat," he said in a defeated voice. "Eat."

While she gorged herself on the entire contents, hams, quarts of milk, oranges, and pears disappearing down that slavering maw, he noticed a letter attached to her filthy burlap dress. He unpinned it and read:

My Dear Mr. Carew:
 We have failed.
 We are sending Mrs. Carew back to you in this most irregular manner, but we can be forgiven because she has proved to be a most irregular guest.
 Her first couple of days here were tranquil, and she seemed to be responding to the diet and treatment, not losing, but not gaining. When we started our program of injections we met our Waterloo. She was given injections of the urine of pregnant sheep, long proven as an appetite-depressant by Dr. Gunter Untervesh, the eminent Swiss dietologist. In her case it proved the exact opposite. She went berserk, screaming, "I want to eat a pregnant sheep!" and burst out of Last Chance looking for one. In her fury she smashed down the barbed wire fence, and when Dietering, a guard dog, bit her in the leg she bit him back. He died from shock. For days she wandered out on the desert, and we felt this would be salubrious. There is naught there but scorpions and sidewinders, and we presumed she would come back to us in desperation sadder, wiser, and surely many pounds slimmer. Nature would do what we could not. She came back... weighing 325 pounds, unbelievably gross, vile, and filled with a malice toward all and a charity toward none that demoralized and frightened our entire staff.
 How did she gain weight in that harsh, virtually lifeless environment? It seemed while in the wilderness she met a man, a certain Euell Gibbons, who opened up new vistas of food consumption for her—cacti, high-bush cranberries, pine trees, goldenrod tea. She also returned with an insatiable craving for Grape-Nuts, and when we

could not supply them to her she flew into a rage, bit the genitals of our cook, which she said tasted like wild hickory nuts, and went on to demonstrate that many parts of a bunkhouse are edible.

So we are regretfully returning her to you in this Brinks truck for reasons of security and besides it was far cheaper than parcel post.

May we suggest immediate psychiatric therapy?

*Yours truly,
Penelope Perkins,
Director of Last Chance Health Farm*

Sated by her binge, she allowed him and Louisiana to push her step by step into the bedroom where she collapsed and slept soundly, her hand still clamped like a vise on the green amulet.

Throughout the day he peeked in to find her still asleep, motionless, only a remnant of her angelic goodness on that blimpish face. He called Dr. Kawpdrayer, stressing the emergency. The psychiatrist stated he was booked solid that afternoon, but agreed to see Colin in his office late that night.

At 9 P.M. he left the house, telling Louisiana he would be back from the psychiatrist's as soon as he could.

"Ain't no doctor gonna be able to help my sweet chile. She done got a hex on her. And old Louisiana knows how to get rid of dem hexes."

A half-hour later Camille awoke, refreshed and ravenous. A nasty smile twisted her fat-swollen lips. A new maniacal flame flashed out of her popping eyes, reddened by veins that seemed to look like tiny pitchforks. "Food!"

It was the croak of a frog coming out of her throat. "Food! Food! Come on, tarbaby, lay a mess o' grits on me."

Louisiana gave her a puzzled look. "Hominy?"

"How do I know how many? As many as you can make. I'm starving. And give me fritters. Cornbread. Fried chicken, basted with the greasiest oil you can find. If necessary take it right out of the crankcase of my Fiat."

"Later, sweet chile, but first I wants yo' to come up to mah room and I gonna fix yo' hex real good."

Only an individual as powerful as Louisiana could have dragged the monstrous Camille out of bed and guided her up the stairs, each step groaning in pain from their combined avoirdupois. "Jes' another step, mah baby, jes' another step. Tha's fine. We here."

She eased Camille into her big brass bed. From a drawer she took out a bongo drum and placed it at Camille's feet. Then she went into her closet and removed a cage. "I done been savin' dis for yo' all day." There was a flurry inside the cage, the sound of squawking. She slid open a door and reached in, pulled out by the feet a large, angry, white rooster. "Come out, yo' mothuhpeckuh," she said to the fowl. With a razor she cut its throat and a font of blood gushed out of the gaping wound, the chicken kicking in its death throes.

"Dem modem doctors doan know nuthin', but old Louisiana, she got the blood of witchdoctors from Africa in her veins. Mah great-granddaddy was de boss witch doctor of all o' dem. He brought his magic to de West Indies, and mah mammy done teached it to me."

She began to draw rolling riffs from the bongo and broke into an ancient chant that might have originated in the grass huts of the Congo.

> *"Spirit of de jungle, spirit down in hell,*
> *Do do dat voodoo dat you do so well,*
> *Send dat feelin' up my sweet chile's spine,*
> *De same old witchcraft when yo' eyes meet mine,*
> *It's dat old debbil moon dat you stole from de skies,*
> *It's dat old debbil moon in her eyes,*
> *But don't change a hair for her,*
> *Not if you care for her,*
> *Stay, little valentine—"*

She stopped, cursing herself. "Aw, shit, I done got into de wrong chant." Then she resumed.

> "Pardon me, boy, is dat de Chattanooga juju?
> Track twenty-nine, and you can give me a shine.
> Cast out de demon and set her free,
> 'Cause she's in between de debbil and de deep blue sea!"

She bent over Camille, whose eyes seemed fascinated by the mumbo-jumbo, swung the chicken over her mistress's head, and screamed, "Hit de road, Jack, and doan yo' come back, no mo', no mo', no mo', no mo'."

She whispered to Camille, "Is dat hex done gone, sweet chile?"

Camille smiled sweetly. "Why, Louisiana, I feel wonderful. Oh, let me put my arms around you and kiss you." They whipped around the maid's neck...

Two blocks away from 54 Dovedroppings, Colin heard the long, horrible scream that violated the serene suburban night. He pushed the accelerator to the floor and made it home in ten seconds, screeching to a stop under his carport. Something had told him the source of the terror was his house. He rushed into Camille's bedroom. "Camy, baby, are you all right?" He flicked on the light. Froze. She was lying there, her eyes shut, one hand on Captain Hardy (were those green eyes winking in wickedness?), the other holding a bunch of white chicken feathers, her mouth smeared with blood. "Camy, what have you eaten?" he cried.

Her eyes opened. That mouth spoke. "I just ate Chicken Little... and the sky is falling." She laughed her sickening laugh. And spit the rooster's comb into his face. "Use that for your dandruff, sweetie."

"Louisiana! For God's sake come down here. She's 'round the bend again." No answer. "Louisiana!" He charged upstairs into her room. The awful sight tore at his eyes. It was a charnelhouse of blood and feathers. A bongo drum with a hole punched through its taut hyena skin. Her dresser overturned. The front of the TV smashed in. And the window. The window! My God, it was completely blown out!

He looked into the garden. There were the Rosenblatts and the Hendersons in their bathrobes, pointing flashlights at something large and dark lying on the tulip beds.

It was the body of Louisiana.

six

The body had been removed by three sweating orderlies; the ambulance, patrol cars, and horrified neighbors were all gone. Colin, wearing two pairs of orange slacks and no pullover, sat smoking cigarette after cigarette. How could this have happened? What could have possessed dear Louisiana to take a header from the upper-floor window? Or was she pushed? And if so, by whom? Who had the strength for such a grisly endeavor? He shuddered. A dark suspicion was forming in his mind.

Outside the wind howled... *You know who... you know who... isn't it obvious?*

"Shut up," he said to the wind and lit another cigarette. From the bedroom came Camille's voice, hoarse and sly, singing, "Food, glorious food," then saying, "Oliver, can I have a bite of your Twist?" The grandfather's clock in the hallway chimed 1 A.M.

A knock at the door. Colin jumped up to answer. He saw in the driveway a 1954 Plymouth, battered and rusty. The man standing in the doorway was of medium height, slightly stooped over, and wearing a rumpled raincoat. "Uh, pardon me, Mr. Carew, for intruding at this late hour, but I got a few questions to ask."

"Questions?"

The man flashed a badge.

"Very well, come in, Lieutenant, er ...."

"That's Lieutenant Christopho, like in Columbus, sir. Hey, that's a nice looking Mercedes you got out there. Could

I ask you a personal question? How much does a thing like that cost? 'Course it's none of my business and you don't have to answer..."

"I don't mind. Fifteen thou."

"Geez, that's a lot of dough. I always wanted one of those things, but when you're only making twelve thousand a year you stay in the Plymouth class."

Colin led the policeman into the living room.

"Ohhhh, this is beautiful, lovely living room. And that sectional couch with the matching loveseat. Magnificent. Now I hope you don't mind me asking this... you don't have to answer if you don't want... but, uh, how much they cost?"

"About two thousand dollars," Colin said.

"Worth every penny. Lovely. And that high-pile Wilton carpet. Terrific stuff. You don't mind my asking... . uh, how much was that?"

"Another two thousand, I'd say."

"Including the foam-rubber padding?"

"That was two hundred extra."

"Well, Mr. Carew, I guess that's all I ready wanted to ask you. Sorry to have troubled you." He got up, walked to the door, picked up a vase, and turned it around in his hands.

Colin said, "That's three hundred dollars."

Lt. Christopho replaced the vase on the table, started out the door, and then stopped. "Gee, I almost forgot. There was one question. Almost slipped my mind. Who killed the spade?"

"Killed? Who said she was killed?"

"Well, was there any reason for her to commit suicide?"

Colin hesitated. Lied. "Well, I don't know, but lately she was acting a little down. Worried about my sick wife."

"Oh, your wife is sick. Geez, that's too bad. Could I see her?"

"I think she's sleeping now."

From the bedroom boomed a basso voice singing:

> *"I've gotta eat, not merely survive,*
> *I've gotta eat ten times a day to keep me alive,*
> *I've gotta eat meat,*

> *I've gotta eat meat,*
> *Corned beef on rye,*
> *Or else I will die,*
> *I gotta eat meat!"*

"That's your wife, Mr. Carew?"

"Yes," Colin said nervously.

"Who did you marry, Ezio Pinza?"

"As I stated, Lieutenant, she's been very ill. Sore throat. That's what accounts for the deep voice."

"Oh sure, I know how bad that can be. Here's how I cure my sore throats." He pulled a lollipop out of that rumpled raincoat and licked it. "I always carry one. Got it from a cop on television, a lollipop cop." He chuckled at his little joke.

"Anything else, Lieutenant?"

"No more tonight. I know it's late. But do me a favor. Don't move out of the neighborhood. We're still investigating."

He opened the door. "Gee, Mr. Carew, my wife is a big Giggling Gourmet fan. Could I have an autograph? Got a pencil here some place. Oh, here." He pulled out a well-worn stub. "Just write it on my rumpled raincoat. I never have it cleaned anyway."

Colin scribbled on the back of the coat.

"Oh, by the way, Mr. Carew. There was one thing that was a little out of the ordinary. I just came from the autopsy. That maid of yours must have been built funny."

"She was rather large."

"No, that's not what I mean. When we got her undressed we were a trifled surprised. You see, her ass was turned completely around. It was facing the front of her body."

"You're joshing..."

"Nope, I saw it with my own eyes. There they were, two gigantic buttocks where the belly should have been, the lower half of the body turned a hundred eighty degrees around, the navel right above the coccyx."

Colin paused. "Perhaps it happened when poor Louisiana fell. The impact can be very jarring."

"You might have a point there. I myself don't know too much about these things, but it seems to me that a body falling twenty feet might break a leg or two and might even incur a fatal concussion. But somehow I don't think that landing in a bed of tulips would cause that kind of catastrophic physiological change. Of course, I'm just a humble little lieutenant making twelve grand a year and no doctor, but in order for that phenomenon... that's the right word, isn't it?"

"Yes."

"Gee, you British guys know everything. Well, in order for that phenomenon to occur it would call for the ripping of some of the body's major muscles. The iliopsoas, the internal oblique, the external oblique, the recotus abdominalis, the transversalis, not to mention the latissimus dorsi, the transecting of the spinal column between the third and fourth lumbar. Plus the gluteus maximus, medius, and minimus, a system known to doctors as the tuchas majoris."

"Lieutenant, your anatomical knowledge is quite astute. Were you pre-med?"

"Nah, I got it off of *General Hospital*. I watch a lot of TV." He gave a suck on his lollipop. "So that lets out the possibility of an accident. Then there's the other thing I found."

"Other thing?"

"Geez, a little car like that is fifteen grand? Oh, excuse me. Yeah, you see, uh, around the waist I saw these great fingermarks dug deeply into the deceased's epidermis, which leads me to a theory that a person of extraordinary strength could have turned her body around. Now you were at the psychiatrist's office when the mishap occurred—I checked that out—and there was nobody else in the house except your wife."

"Who is sick," Colin added quickly.

"Yeah, sick, that's right. And even if she wasn't sick I'm sure that a mere slip of a girl could never rip a two-hundred-fifty-pound human up like that. Maybe it was a burglar or a team of burglars. You know, three of them holding the top half of the body while the other three turned the lower half completely around. Of course, uh, I don't know why burglars would want to do that. That's not their thing, but there are a lot of weirdos around."

They heard a noise in the hallway, the sound of pounding footsteps often associated with the walk of a leviathan.

Camille stalked by on her way to the kitchen, huge, menacing, her eyes lit by that unholy light.

"Oh, hello, darling," Colin said lightly. "This is Lieutenant Christopho."

"Geez, it's a pleasure to make your acquaintance, Mrs. Carew. Hope you feel better."

She glowered at him, said nothing, and continued into the kitchen.

"Sorry about that Ezio Pinza crack, Mr. Carew. I think you married Orson Welles. As I was saying, it would have to be a person with enormous strength, someone—"

Camille came back, bearing the GE refrigerator in her arms. And disappeared into the bedroom. They heard the sound of smacking lips and gurgling.

"Someone like, uh, your wife, someone who's strong enough to pick up a half-ton, eighteen-cubic-foot refrigerator."

"Wait a minute. It's only a sixteen-cubic-footer. And only half full."

"Well, since she was the only one in the house with the victim and she does have that kind of strength, I feel obligated to at least make note of it in my report." He stuck his hand into another pocket of that rumpled raincoat, and extracted a handful of water. "Geez, it's rumpled rain! Maybe I oughta get this thing cleaned." Then he found his notepad and worked the stubby pencil on it, murmuring, "Wife built like tractor, has fantastic strength, ability to lift refrigerators..."

Colin lowered his head. "Lieutenant, are you positively ruling out an accident?"

"You can't be positive about anything in this crazy world, but based on my solving hundreds of murder cases

I'd say the chances of an accident were rather remote. So, that little Mercedes in the driveway is fifteen thousand dollars, huh? Son of a gun."

"You like that car?"

"Sure do. But when you make twelve Gs a year—" He threw out his hands helplessly, smiled his adorably humble smile.

"You know," said Colin, "I always had a mad desire to own a battered, rusty 1954 Plymouth. What say we swap? You take the Mercedes, give me the Plymouth."

"Gee, I don't know, Mr. Carew. The department frowns on that kind of thing."

"Supposing I throw in the couch and the loveseat?"

"The couch *and* the loveseat?"

"Plus the carpeting."

"Okay. You got a deal." He scribbled on his notepad, murmuring aloud, "It is my considered opinion that the death which occurred at the domicile on 54 Dovedroppings Lane was due to a precipitous fall during which the deceased hit an abnormally hard tulip bed thus resulting in the turning about of the lower extremities. Cause of demise: Accident." He pumped

Colin's hand warmly. "Good night, Mr. Carew, it's been a pleasure to meet you and the lovely Mrs. Carew."

From the bedroom came an animal-like roaring and the clicking of teeth.

Lt. Christopho, his new car key in his hand, went to the door, then turned. "Uh, one last.. ."

"Take the vase," Colin said. The officer did and left. Good fellow, this Christopho, Colin mused. Certainly no Serpico, but a good fellow nevertheless.

But now there was the confirmed horror of Camille, his dear wife, transformed into this voracious maniac of a thing.

And the wind outside, strangely sounding like Al Jolson, whispered... *You ain't seen nothin' yet...*

seven

When the black Cadillac bearing the MD plates pulled into the Carew driveway, the hotline between the Hendersons and the Rosenblatts and the Tartaglias and others who owned Country Clubbers on Dovedroppings Lane came alive. Doctors, not one but two, the voices said. Maybe they can do something for poor Camille, something...

And the winds whispered... *That's horror... oh boy, two doctors... the bill alone is horror...*

Drs. Mark Twine and Sigmund Kawpdrayer met a pale Colin at the door and were ushered in. In his angst, he had dressed so quickly he had stuck his legs into the sleeves of the orange pullover and was trying to work the fawn slacks over his head, but they corrected him.

"I have invited Dr. Twine to assist me in the event medication is needed," the psychiatrist said, giving his goatee a thoughtful stroke and then stroking Dr. Twine's moustache as well.

"Thanks," said Dr. Twine. "I needed that. Lead the way, Colin."

Before they even reached the bedroom their noses began to wrinkle with distaste. The scent of body fat and moldering food should have prepared them for what they were about to witness. But professionals though they were, they still started at the sight. Camille, more monstrous and menacing than ever, loomed like an alp out of the filthy, food-spattered bed piled high with empty cereal boxes, aluminum panikins, soda bottles, cracker crumbs, dried oatmeal lumps. The mad, sick eyes had forced their way out of the swollen face and alternately popped out and retracted as though on pogo sticks. Near the bed stood what was left of the GE, its doors and shelves tom up and scattered like leaves.

"So the general practitioner and the shrink have joined forces to take me on..." The croak was back in the throat, a defiant curl on the bloated lips. "I fear neither of you. To me you're just small potatoes." The eyes suddenly flashed. "Yes, yes, give me small potatoes! Lots of small potatoes—French fried, home fried, baked, boiled, Julienne..."

"No, no!" Colin began to shake. "I can't feed you any more. Your heart will soon collapse from all the weight and you'll die."

But Dr. Kawpdrayer said soothingly, "Give her what she wants. It will make her more tractable, calm, pliant." And Colin went to the kitchen to prepare it.

"You are clever, Viennese psychiatrist," mocked the voice. "But I shall play the game with you. I will find it amusing."

"There's no game, Camille," the psychiatrist said in a light, even tone. "We just dropped in to keep tabs on you, that's all."

"Tabs!" Camille rose like some huge angry bear. "Tabs! I hate Tabs! They have only one calorie in every six ounces. No, give me the real thing, the fattening, sugar-saturated Coke!" And she sang in that rumbling voice, "I'd like to buy the world a Coke and make the whole world fat!"

"My God," said Dr. Twine.

"Injection," said Dr. Kawpdrayer. "She must be tranquillized immediately. One hundred milligrams of Calmazine."

But when Dr. Twine attempted to locate the vein she sent him tumbling with a backhanded blow.

"Camille." Now Dr. Kawpdrayer's voice had a teasing quality in it. "This"—he held up a bag of Campfire marshmallows—"for the injection."

Camille grunted a surly assent to the trade-off and permitted the needle to slip in. Ate the marshmallows one by one, sucking and slurping, then spat the cellophane into Dr. Twine's face. But then the dosage began to work and she slipped into a dreamy mood, her hand fondling the jade amulet as though it were the genitals of a lover.

"She's receptive," Dr. Kawpdrawer said softly. He pulled out of his weskit a large gold pocketwatch. "Camille, watch this watch." He swayed it gently; it rocked like a pendulum. "See this watch... I am going to hypnotize you... look at the face, look at the hands, look how shiny it is... it's making... you... sleepy... sleepy... happy... grumpy... dopey. Your eyelids are getting heavier... heavier... you are falling deeper asleep... deeper..." As he droned, he himself, Dr. Twine, and Colin all suddenly pitched to the floor in a stupor. Camille shrugged, leaned over, grasped and ate the watch.

Some minutes later Dr. Kawpdrayer awoke and roused the other sleepers. "Refreshing, wasn't it? Now we make a new start." He repeated the hypnotic phrases, using in place of the watch a key ring, and it sent her into a state of quiescence.

"Good. Now, Camille, tell me. You seem to be very fond of that figurine. What do you call it?"

"Captain Hardy."

"May I speak to him?"

"Oh, yes."

"Figurine, will you speak to me?"

"Yes." The tone was muffled, ugly.

"So your name is Captain Hardy."

"No, my name is Captain Spaulding, the African explorer." Strangely the voice went from low register to the higher-pitched, lecherous voice of Groucho Marx. "Ah, Lydia, Lydia, we can't go on meeting like this."

Dr. Kawpdrayer said, "My name is not Lydia."

"It's not? Then that's another reason we can't go on meeting like this."

"Ach, you try my patience."

"No," said the Groucho voice, "you try my patients. The medical board has me up for malpractice. And that's the nastiest remark I ever hoid. Ah, come away with me, doctor, and we'll do mad passionate things. We'll dance to dawn. And if Dawn isn't around we'll dance to some other rock group, the Rolling Stones, Chicago, the Who. Anyone you want. You're paying for it." And Camille's hand started to flick at an imaginary Groucho cigar, the eyes rolled up, the brows lifted puckishly. Then it happened.

A thick, grease-pencil black moustache materialized on her upper lip. Stayed there for three seconds. And just as mysteriously vanished!

"This new personality of Camille's seems to have remarkable flexibility of vocal tones, gestures, and facial mutations," he noted to his colleague. Then to Camille: "May I have the Hardy voice back?"

"Sure thing. But first, dad, can we go into your study for a man-to-man talk? I think I got Polly Benedict in trouble..."

Dr. Kawpdrayer was nonplussed. "You are Captain Hardy?"

"Oh, I thought you meant Andy Hardy," Camille laughed. Then the voice changed back into that horrifying roar and from her mouth the smell of Skippy peanut butter spread over the room like an evil cloud. "Yes, psychiatric schweinhund. What do you wish?"

"Are you within Camille?"

"Yes."

"Are you speaking for her?"

"Yes."

"Do you control her?"

"Yes."

"Why are you possessing her?"

"On the advice of counsel and at this point in time I must respectfully decline to answer... to the best of my recollection..."

"What kind of an answer is that?"

"I don't know, but it works in Washington."

As the questioning proceeded, Captain Hardy's answers for the most part evasive as though he were having his joke at the psychiatrist's expense, Colin was lured from the bedroom by the insistent burring of the phone in his den.

The voice was tinny, far off. "Hello, Colin. Babs Pish-Tepple here."

"Babs, my luv. How good of you to ring."

"I've a spot of bad news, Colin. It's Roderick."

"Roderick? Good heaven, what happened?"

"It's a long story but basically it all started when he came back from mucking about with you in ruddy old Tibet. Seemed haunted, kept washing his hands as though he'd touched something frightfully disgusting. Grew morose. Uncommunicative. Developed an insatiable appetite."

"Do go on."

"So much so that Roderick began to grow huge, almost womanly appendages. The old tits, you know. They proved his undoing. Today we were at Epsom Downs high above the stands in Lord Beavereater's private box."

"I know her," Colin said. "Pray continue." He could still hear the bantering between Dr. Kawpdrayer and Camille in a private comer of his ear.

"It was the match race," Babs said, "between the Russian horse, Proletariat, and the Iranian-Israeli entry, that noble stallion, Shah Shtill. There they were, neck and neck, pounding down the stretch, old Roderick like an excited child up on his feet, bending to get a better look—and then..."

"I know," Colin said quietly. "His massive breasts pulled him out of the box and onto the turf three hundred feet below."

"How did you know?"

"There's quite a bit of that going round." Now Colin, numb, frozen, shocked at the death of his old companion, nevertheless found a hidden reserve of strength and bravely asked, "Who won?"

"Oh, Proletariat, of course," Babs trilled gaily. "Had a tidy sum on his nose. Paid for old Roderick's funeral with enough left over for a life of total splendor."

"Capital! Glad to hear it. Was Johnnie Merridew saddled up?"

"Rode the winner as a matter of fact."

"Good show. Fine lad, Merridew, magnificent hands. Who rode Shah Shtill?"

"Parker."

"Little Philbert Parker? Still riding at his age?"

"No more, I'm afraid. Had a nasty spill at the finish line and was shot with his horse."

"Pity. Who shot him?"

"Merridew."

"Smashing. Well, Babs, thanks so much for calling." He hung up. Shook his head. Poor Roderick gone. And that terrible weight gain. Like Camille's. But why?

He reentered the bedroom to pick up the rest of the interrogation. Saw the psychiatrist leaning forward, almost face to face with his subject, addressing the rasping voice. "Who are you, Captain Hardy?"

"That's for me to know and you to find out. Ess, ess."

"Why are you in her body?"

"To punish her. Ess, ess."

"Ah," the psychiatrist said. "It is speaking German, telling her to 'eat, eat.' "

"Noooooo," the voice croaked. "Not ess, ess. I am saying the initials SS. Familiar, no?"

The psychiatrist paled. "I know nothing of these letters SS. I was working for the underground. I am Viennese, not German."

Camille thrust her arm up quickly. "Sieg heil!" Unconsciously the psychiatrist leaped up, clicked his heels, and his own right arm jabbed out. He yanked it down nervously, a guilty look on his face.

"Ha, ha!" the voice croaked. "You were in the SS. Even now your blood-group tattoo itches in your left armpit. You are Reichsführer Klaus Schoogmann, wanted for war crimes."

A rage swept over the unmasked Kawpdrayer. "You have betrayed me. You shall die!" He lunged at Camille, screaming German obscenities.

But she caught him by the throat, held him for a few agonizing seconds, and hurled him out of the bedroom window. He landed with a bounce that rocked the garden and gave a death scream that could be heard for many blocks.

While Dr. Twine rushed out to administer whatever aid he could, Colin slowly dialed the police.

As Lt. Christopho poked about in the garden, Colin, dumbstruck and bone-weary, sat shoving Tootsie Rolls into Camille's mouth and shivered each time those tumescent lips smacked. Sated at last, she closed those popped-out eyes and slipped into slumber.

The lieutenant walked into the house, still in that rumpled raincoat. "Uh, pardon me for letting myself in, but I didn't want to disturb you. Listen, that kraut psychiatrist out there is dead."

"Good Lord," Colin breathed.

"Awful sight. Fingermarks etched deeply into his throat. Must have taken someone with a lot of strength to do him in."

"Why do you say that?"

"Because," and he paused for emphasis, "the head was turned completely around. Either that or he put his jacket on backwards. Anyway, do you suppose there's anybody around here capable of doing that?"

"Just me and poor Camille. Still sick, you know."

"Sure, sure. Oh, before I forget, I gotta tell you my wife and I are really enjoying that Mercedes. And she loves the couch and the loveseat. We sit on them all the time while we're watching *Police Story*. It's about time they showed the true agony of honest cops on television. But tell me, sir, what kind of drapes oughta go with that couch?"

"This may come as a shock to you, Lieutenant, but the ones in our living room are a perfect match."

"Yeah, that's what I thought. You know something else? If I'm driving the Mercedes my wife needs a car too. I saw that cute little Fiat 850 out front. If you don't mind my asking, what's a car like that cost? Not that it's any of my business..."

"Three, four thousand. It has extras."

"Too much money for a cop who only draws twelve Gs a year. Well, let's fill out this homicide report."

Colin reached into his pocket, pulled out the Fiat keys and dropped them into Lt. Christopho's palm.

"Uh," the officer grinned, hitting himself on the head. "Funny how your mind plays games with you. Did I say homicide? I meant accident." He scribbled furiously, and pointedly said out loud, "It is my considered opinion that the deceased died of a fall into a particularly heavy petunia, thus causing the head to rotate one hundred eighty degrees. Cause of death: accident."

Colin pointed to the drapes. "They unhook from the top."

Dr. Twine, still clutched by the terror, lurched back into the house. "Colin, whatever this thing is, it's beyond the realm of medicine and psychiatry. But there may be a greater power..."

"I don't think Sinatra would be interested in this sort of business."

"No, I mean... uh... are you religious?"

"Not particularly. Why?"

"There's an evil presence wracking that poor girl. Perhaps if you called in a clergyman..."

And outside the winds whispered... *Oh wow... now we're getting into the heavy stuff... the clergy... that horror had better watch its ass... the clergy is coming!*

Romaine LeLane vaulted out of a deep sleep. The Hindu bed of nails he habitually slept upon to insure the proper circulation of blood shook as he sprang. His heart thumped wildly. What had torn him from that splendid dream of running through a field of low-calorie, organically fertilized endives, then kneeling by a mountain brook to sip ice-cold unfluoridated water? Was it some evil spirit defiling his domicile? That horror that had been gnawing at him for the past few nights, faceless and nameless?

He looked about his humbly furnished beach house for the source of the noise. No ghoul, no monster, just an industrious burglar rifling his dresser drawer and throwing some personal effects into a sack.

"Oh, that," LeLane laughed, his tension gone. Whereupon his stunning collection of muscle and bone launched an uppercut that broke the man's face into several pieces.

He jumped back onto the bed of nails and resumed dreaming.

eight

Because he and Camille had no formal religious affiliation in the community (he was a lapsed Quaker, she an atheist—not an orthodox one, but reformed), Colin was not certain which clergyman to bring in and decided to play it safe and telephone them all. And the following night at nine the entire Levittown Inter-Faith Council came—Dr. Romilar Desmond, the Episcopalian, Rabbi Bindlebinder, chubby and cheerful as usual, and Father Blatty. The latter seemed to be especially concerned. When Colin had given him, as he did the others, a long and detailed account of her malady—the revolting accretion of weight, the unaccountable profanities, the vast range of new voices, the immense strength, the failure to respond to medical and psychiatric care—Father Blatty, recalling a sinister, mind-bending experience he had witnessed long ago in Georgetown, muttered, "Oh no."

They trooped into the bedroom, each prepared to call upon his own special knowledge. When she saw them enter, Camille broke into the maddened laugh of a hyena. "Ah, the men of the cloth have arrived!" She reared up, ready to do battle, her tongue whipping about like the tail of a scorpion, the voice even deeper. "Come, gentlemen, let us begin."

Dr. Desmond came right to the point. "You, you who lurk within Camille. You have thrown out little hints about yourself. You express a peculiar fondness for devil's food cake, as we noted at the Henderson party. You are aroused by deviled eggs. Now tell us. Are you the devil?"

From deep within that mass of hideous fat came a rumble like a Vesuvius come to life. A cloud of hellfire was belched out, mixed attractively with the scent of Heinz ketchup. But the voice spoke not.

"Come, tell us," Father Blatty demanded. "This is no time to fudge."

"Fudge, fudge!" Camille—or whatever it was, for they found it difficult to call this misshapen horror Camille any more—jumped up, shaking the bed with her gross tonnage. "Yes, I want fudge! Chocolate fudge, vanilla fudge..."

Colin, by now an old hand at placating her, rushed into the kitchen and came back with a plate full of sickeningly sweet chocolate squares.

Camille's rasping voice mutated with celerity. It was now that of the immortal black entertainer, Pigmeat Markham. "Here come de fudge... here come de fudge!" She crushed the squares into one huge lump and rammed it into her mouth, mewing and barking and braying and bleating.

"You, you who have been called Captain Hardy," the priest pushed on. "Are you the Father of Evil, the Prince of Darkness, Satan?"

"No," the now-returned rasping voice boomed. "He is at present in Washington, that 'sinister force' the administration was speaking about. He who altered tapes and made documents disappear."

"But you are," interrupted the rabbi, "some kind of lesser spirit or dybbuk, as we refer to it in my faith?"

"Yes."

"What kind?" asked Father Blatty. "How are you called?"

"The same way you are. First the area code, then the number, and if you dial before 8 A.M. it's only a dollar."

"It has a certain wit," the minister noted.

"A devilish wit," retorted the furry voice.

"What is your name?" the priest kept hammering away.

"I have many names... Le Glouton, Le Grande Bouffe, Gros Mangeur, Chauser, Fresser. In certain slum areas of New York I am known as Fat, Fat, the Water Rat."

Rabbi Bindlebinder became excited. "Fresser? That means big eater in Yiddish. And chauser means pig, you should pardon the expression."

"I am the demon of gluttony," the voice thundered pridefully. "It is I who make all creatures overeat themselves into fat, slovenly wretches."

The trio began a low-pitched but heated discussion between themselves. Clearly some kind of strategy was called for.

They broke the huddle and Rahbi Bindlebinder resumed the questioning. "You expect us to believe this absurd tale?"

"I can prove it if I want to," the voice croaked smugly.

"Do so," said the rabbi.

"Listen," and the voice changed from its basso register to that of a woman, an immigrant woman pleading in broken English. "Oh, Zalman, my boy. Eat your noodle pudding. Eat, eat; they're starving in Europe."

"My God." Rabbi Bindlebinder fell back, his skullcap tumbling off his head. "That was my mother's voice. She always said that, 'They're starving in Europe.' And because of that I ate enough for Latvia, Lithuania, and half of Poland, which accounts for my corpulence. But I swear, tomorrow the diet starts; this time for sure."

"They all say that," the thing in Camille said contemptuously. Then sneered. "That's one for the demon, nothing for the Jewish kid," now in a Don Rickles voice.

Thank heaven she sneered, and didn't snicker, Colin thought. That would have reminded her of you know what and I'm fresh out. All I have left is a few Milky Ways and a Mars Bar.

On a hunch Father Blatty said, "If you are so clever a demon doubtless you can speak in any tongue."

"Tongue, tongue! Yes, I want tongue!" the demon screamed. "Tongue on rye, tongue on pumpernickel and hold the mayo. On second thought, give me lots of mayo. That's where the calories are."

Colin flung the thing a sandwich, it wolfed it down, burped, and said, "Resume, Papist swine."

"Do you know how to speak Latin?"

"Simplicity itself. *Lesbia est puella. Catullus est puer.*"

"Hmmm," the impressed priest said. "It speaks a very classical, almost Vatican-like Latin."

"Yes, I do, Father. And if you dig Latin how's about this? 'Ixnay on the ullshitbay.' "

Father Blatty seemed confused until Rabbi Bindlebinder, himself an old street boy, said. "That's *pig* Latin, again you should pardon the expression."

"Oh, Father," the voice now was seductive, intriguing. "May I whisper something to you?" Father Blatty moved in, eager to learn some secret that would unlock the door to this girl's tormented soul. Suddenly it gave a roar of triumph and vomited a stream of thick green matter onto his black priest's suit. He pulled back, his entire front awash with the green stuff. It looked like pea soup. And when a label, Lipton's, slipped out of Camille's mouth, he realized it was.

"Look," the demon jested. "The trademark of your priestly calling has been soiled by my devilish vomit." The voice changed quickly; it was now that of that revolting little kid on TV jeering, "Ring around the collar... ring around the collar!"

"How long have you been wreaking your havoc upon mankind?" Dr. Desmond said to the croaking persona.

"As long as man has been upon earth," it said. "Didn't Eve eat the apple?"

"You were in Eden?" Dr. Desmond asked.

"I had a garden apartment," the thing stated. "I have always been tempting man. If I had had my way Lot's wife would have been turned to a pillar of lard. When the Children of Israel set up the Golden Calf, I almost had them convinced that they should eat it. At the Last Supper all they wanted to do was to send out for cold cuts. I said, no, let's put up a sweet table."

The three men of faith huddled again, convinced at last this was a bona fide, A-1, card-carrying demon. They broke out of the huddle, grim-faced and determined.

"Then," said Father Blatty, acting as spokesman, "we shall launch an assault against you to the very core of your rotten being. We shall vanquish you, cast you out, for in union there is strength. We shall face you with a united, unbreakable front of religious fervor."

The thing in Camille hooted and howled. "United, are you? Let us see how united." Then it spoke. Spoke in the polished tones of Dr. Romilar Desmond. "Why should we support the Israelis? The Arabs have the oil, and besides Jerusalem is a Christian city."

Rabbi Bindlebinder turned his head quickly to the Episcopalian. "Did you say that?"

"No, no," Dr. Desmond protested. "The voice came from the demon. You know it has the power of vocal reproduction."

"Yes, and also the power to reach into another's mind. Which means you *did* say it."

"All right, I did say it. My God, man... and, uh, your God too... we must face the realities of the Middle East."

"And what are those realities?" the rabbi said with asperity. "The destruction of the only democracy there? You see? In the crunch, goyim always sell us out."

"Well, dammit," Dr. Desmond fired back. "You did kill Christ."

"We?" The rabbi was livid. "Who crucified in those days? Jews? No. Romans? Yes."

"Wait a minute!" interjected Father Blatty. "Let's not be so fast to jump on the Romans. After all, they were the first Christians."

"And the best, I suppose," Dr. Desmond said sarcastically. "Corrupt popes, indulgences, orgies..."

"Which you highborn Wasps corrected, of course," Father Blatty jabbed back. "You and your Protestants with witch trials in Salem, putting people in stocks. I'm sick of this, Dr. Desmond. I wash my hands of the whole affair."

"A true Pontius Pilate," sneered Dr. Desmond. "The going gets tough and you wash your hands."

From the demon: a gloating on the malformed face. "Gentlemen," Rabbi Bindlebinder said anxiously. "We're letting this get out of hand."

"Don't interrupt a friendly discussion between two Christian soldiers, matzoh-face," Dr. Desmond said snippily.

"Matzoh-face? Look how Mr. Whitebread is talking," the rabbi said, more to himself than anyone else.

Then the dam burst and there were arguments and cries of "deicide," "popery," "leftfooter," the demon all the while cackling at the top of its head.

"Wait!" Father Blatty had come back to his senses. "Can't you see what's happened here? This... this thing is playing the old divide-and-conquer gambit. I shall face him alone!" He turned to do so. At that very moment the demon altered its voice, the fumes of cheap muscatel and a thousand flophouses issued from its body, and it croaked mockingly: "Couldja help an old altar boy, Faddah?"

That voice! The voice that had haunted him in a million nightmares! Father Blatty threw his hands into the air, gasped, and fell in a faint on the floor.

The minister and rabbi pulled him out of the bedroom into the cool sweetness of the front lawn, where he revived. Colin saw the three clergymen exchange guilty looks, and bow their heads.

Before they walked off, the priest, his face a mask of melancholia, said apologetically, "I have had past experiences with demons, but this thing in Camille is too strong. It must be exorcised, but as you can see, we are not the ones capable of such a task. I'm sorry, Colin, but you must look elsewhere for a savior."

A long and hideous laugh rang out of the bedroom and flew all over the neighborhood. And hundreds of already unnerved Levittowners shook in their beds. And their pets, the first to have sensed the horror that now engulfed this peaceful place, said to themselves, *that did it,* bolted out of the Country Clubbers as though deserting Noah's Ark, and in a long line they headed out of the community—

dogs, cats, ants, parakeets, hamsters, gerbils, and a turtle on whose back was lettered "Don't Blame Me; I Voted for McGovern"—all streaming down Route One toward Trenton, snarling traffic for miles.

Colin wearily trudged back into the bedroom. Camille, a broad smile on her ghastly face indicating her satisfaction with the wrecking job on the clergy, lay fast asleep. And now, he thought, what was left? She—or it—had routed the minions of medicine, psychiatry, religion, had committed two ghastly murders (he reconsidered the Nazi's death; all right, one ghastly murder and one justifiable homicide), had scorned the one thing most sacred, his own love. And now it sat triumphant over the scene, daring any and all comers.

Father Blatty had spoken of a savior. But in view of the demon's inpenetrability, did such a champion exist? Was there anyone who could drive away the awful billows of disgusting fat? Who could literally make a molehill out of a mountain? It had to be someone whose burning mission in life was to rid the world of this demon of gluttony. Someone with strength, courage, and experience who would know how to battle it blow for blow, trick for trick...

And Colin Carew, the not-so-Giggling Gourmet anymore, knew where her last hope for salvation lay.

III: The End

Man does not live by bread alone.
WELCH'S GRAPE JELLY

Don't fire until you see the whites...
CRISPUS ATTUCKS

There is a sight at which it is not worth peeking,
The sight of Woody Allen streaking.
ANON.

one

Colin paid the cabdriver and walked up the sandy path to the modest white stucco bungalow a few hundred yards from the twinkling Pacific. Checked the mailbox to make sure he had found his man and knew he had from the contents bulging out, copies of *Strength & Health* magazine, a catalogue from a discount vitamin house in Chicago, and a sample of a new toothpaste made entirely out of beef jerky.

He knocked at the door. Romaine LeLane, The Exerciser, opened it and peered out angrily. "Why have you come? I told you on the phone last night nothing about you concerns or interests me, you hedonist, you pusher of obesity, you..." And started to slam it in his face when Colin cried out, "For God's sake, man, you've got to talk to me. You had every right to hang up on me, but this is something bigger than our petty differences."

"Very well," LeLane sighed deeply. "Come in and state your business."

He led the Giggling Gourmet into a parlor furnished only in the barest way, the old sweat-stained exercise mat as the carpet, the Swedish box as the table, and chains hanging from the ceiling on whose ends were rings of steel. "May I offer you some simple refreshments, a glass of turnip tea, a delicious jimsonweed cutlet and a Milkbone, excellent for keeping the teeth and gums conditioned? Not the ornate and rich fare you offer your addled following, perhaps, but these simple foods reflect my basic philosophy."

As Colin nibbled away, cracking a molar on the Milkbone, he wondered, Was Camille eating at this very minute and how was her father—who had agreed to stay with her until he returned—coping with her demonic assaults?

LeLane in the meantime was on his typical routine, bending and stretching, kicking out, running in place, and doing deep breathing exercises, each inhalation into those mighty lungs emptying the room of usable oxygen, forcing Colin to gasp and run to the open window for air.

"Now what is this matter which has you so distraught? Has Philadelphia run out of cream cheese? Boston out of cream pies?" The Exerciser's sarcasm was ill concealed.

Colin spoke, unfolded the entire story, trembling when he came to the sequences of horror and shock. At first LeLane was impassive, but then, swept up by the narrative, he became so engrossed and intense his steely hands squeezed the juice out of a barbell. Then he sighed and shook his head. "Colin, it has always been my feeling that there was some malevolent force in this world, sly, irresistible, and all-powerful, that was engaged in the uglification of man through adiposity. I have felt his presence often, even of late in dreams. But would it not be presumptuous of me, a mere mortal, to tackle this monster when all others have met ignominious failure?" To demonstrate his frustration, LeLane swung his arms out, and in doing so, smashed a gaping hole in each wall.

"No, I think you'll do very nicely," said Colin. "Will you come to Levittown, if not for me, then for poor Camille? You remember how slim and lovely she was, a tribute to all you stand for. Well, here." He opened his attache case and produced several large blowups. "These pictures were taken by me last night. See... see what she has become."

A flush stole up LeLane's neck and onto those leathery cheeks, the bright redness even surfacing through his bronzed features. "Good heavens!" If the man had not possessed such magnificent bodily control he would have retched, Colin knew.

"This." LeLane pointed to the amulet around her neck. "I have seen this face before, I swear it." He beckoned for

Colin to follow him into his library. The Exerciser pulled an old dusty volume down from the top shelf.

"My book of horrors," he explained. "In here are the evidences of what self-indulgence can do." He leafed through it. There were photos of Fatty Arbuckle, King Farouk, fat ladies of the circus. "Poor creatures," he said, "they had no chance against it." He riffled further. "Here, drawings of the Greek gods of Lyssa and Mania, who produced illness, disease, disfigurement, and insanity in man. And—"

Suddenly both men cringed.

There it was on the last page.

A depiction of the giant bulbous-bellied idol whose representation Camille had called Captain Hardy.

"It is the demon of gluttony," LeLane said with a shudder. "The text calls him all the other names you have mentioned, but this is his original name, the name he is known by in Tibet, where he was first seen—Chow Down."

"The cave, the cave!" Colin shouted. "That thing in the cave! Why, I should have known about this long ago... all the way back in Chapter Four..."

"Chow Down was the demonic leader of a cult of gluttony. Which explains how those mandarins died, bloated almost beyond recognition. At his wicked bidding they ate themselves to death. And now he reposes around your wife's neck."

"Wait, if I could just cut off that fiendish figurine."

"Too late," LeLane said dourly. "Chow Down himself is by now within her, part of her every nerve, tissue, and cell. He holds complete sway."

Colin's face fell. "Then there's no hope, even with you in my comer."

LeLane put an arm around this young man he had considered a natural enemy. He said, "There is always hope. I shall come to Levittown."

"Bless you," Colin sobbed, licking his hand, which tasted of fresh-cut alfalfa.

"But you must show me that you have repented, Colin. Quick, do fifty pushups."

Colin did, his blood rushing, his body strained. Now not even Camille was in his thoughts, just a message from every muscle in his body: Quick—the Ben-Gay!

LeLane looked out at the sea. Spoke slowly and profoundly. "This will be a symbolic battle, you understand. And to dramatize it, before I even enter your ill-fated house I must stand outside in my black coat with my black bag silhouetted like an avenging angel in the misty glow of a streetlamp. The demon must know I am there."

"There is no streetlamp outside my house."

"Build one. I shall be there in two days. First I must climb high into the mountains above Malibu and purify myself for the struggle."

And the winds howled from Santa Monica to Levittown... *Now it's coming... the fat fight at the OK Corral... The Exerciser is on his way!*

two

Colin flew back to Philadelphia, the jet making its regulated turn over the Pacific before swinging east, casting a shadow on the Malibu mountains. Down there, he knew, was Romaine LeLane, the last card to be played in this unholy game of man versus demon, with possibly a multi-million-dollar fight against George Foreman for the winner.

As the aircraft climbed to its 37,000-foot cruising level, LeLane, atop a peak, knelt in his rites of purification.

He chanted the word "okra... okra... okra" over and over again.

He whispered entreaties to the spirits of Rodale and Adelle Davis and McFadden.

He held up a can of Shasta Diet Chocolate soda to the sun and watched the rays change it from brown to gold.

He stripped off his clothing and stepped into a large oaken tub containing lime D-Zerta (eight calories per serving) so that it would give his body a glistening, protective shield.

And so that his session in the mountains should not be a total loss, he tore down enough redwood trees to build a rustic lodge that would be the beginnings of a profitable five-hundred-acre summer camp, for man does not live by Hollywood Low-Profile Bread alone.

Thus cleansed, he came down to the valley, packed a number of unusual things in his large black satchel, slipped on a black trenchcoat, and jogged the fifteen miles to the airport.

three

Midnight on Dovedroppings Lane.

The neighbors, assailed for hours on end by a volley of unearthly screams, taunts, and curses, had attempted to go about their nightly rituals with unconcern, watching their favorite TV programs, trying to blot out the hovering horror with booze and seconals, but to no avail. Each show of bravado collapsed quickly with each burst of insanity from Number 54. Henderson, an old National Rifle Association member, fingered the shotgun across his knees. "I don't know what's going on in there, but I'll kill if I have to." Helen cowered in the bedroom corner, knitting a Wallace poster. The Rosenblatts made frantic love on Arnold's latest Sexomatic mattress, hoping the twanging of the springs would distract them from the terror next door.

The street was still as a tomb. Stiller. Stiller and Meara. The only sign of life was under the newly installed streetlamp in front of the Carew house. In its yellowish glow stood a tall man using a spraycan of Arrid Extra-Dry to create his own mysterious and dramatic mist because Mother Nature had forgotten to fill an order for one hundred tons of mist (lean). She was too busy hustling margarine on TV. His black coat and valise glinted in the glow. He was ready for the thing that pulsed inexorably within. He was The Exerciser.

"LeLannnnnnnnne...!" The voice boomed volcanically through the bedroom window far out into the night, and every Levittowner dived under his bed. Henderson's gun went off, sending a hail of buckshot into his leg, but being an old hunter for many years he was used to accidental wounding, even enjoyed it in a strange way. The protracted, demonic scream stopped the Rosenblatts in midorgasm (in midair), and they grabbed their son, rushed into their sports car, and drove to Boston. "We don't know anyone in Boston," complained Rona.

"We're lovely people," Arnold said. "We'll make friends fast."

The Exerciser strode into the bedroom. There was Foster Hamilton, haggard, unshaven, a bottle of Chivas Regal in his hand. And Colin, red-eyed, burnt-out, pacing up and down, mumbling whatever came into his head to keep his sanity—"There has never been a bebop alto player from Irkutsk"... "Iceland has a low national death rate from heat stroke"... "The government of Brazil has never established veterans' hospitals for army ants"—and stopped to berate himself: "Why am I remembering those ridiculous little fillers they print in *The New York Times?* Because I'm going mad, mad, do you hear me? Mad...!"

"I hear you, my beloved husband," croaked the thing that looked like a monstrous, obscene toad dominating the bed. "But now my most formidable adversary has arrived to confront me. Welcome, Romaine LeLane, welcome to my pit of shit." From that slimy, drooling mouth a stream of black viscous material spattered LeLane's face. He winced. *My-T-Fine Chocolate Pudding!* The demon was opening up with its big guns. "You will be pleased to know," it croaked, "that I now weigh three hundred fifty pounds... three hundred fifty pounds, and still rising."

"You say that with relish," LeLane said, then realized his faux pas.

The thing began to yammer, "Relish, I want relish! hotdog relish, watermelon relish..."

Hamilton turned to the old strongman. "Romaine, old buddy, can't you do anything to stop that infernal craving? I think her heart is faltering."

The Exerciser felt for the pulse. A mere fifteen beats a minute. Not good. As he did, the demon's hand swatted him with jackhammer force against the jaw, but drew it back limply, howling in pain. Any ordinary jaw would have been shattered into splinters. Not the granite one that jutted out of the craggy face of The Exerciser. "Damn you, you fucking superman!" Then wheedling, pleading, "Sugar, give me sugar. My body craves sugar."

"You shall have some sweetness," LeLane said coolly.

Colin protested, "No, no more sugar, please. It'll kill her."

"I am going to inject her with a massive dose of saccharin, three hundred ccs. straight into the vein," and he pushed the hypodermic squarely into that thin blue streak.

The demon howled, "I love it because it's sweet, but I hate it because it isn't putting a damn ounce on me. You are a clever bastard, LeLane. But I shall win."

"Oh, that saccharin shot slowed her down," Hamilton exulted. "I think you've found the weak spot, old strongman."

"No," LeLane corrected him. "Chow Down has just been quieted for a moment. But he is powerful, arrogant, cunning..."

"You bet your ass I am," the demon said in the voice of H. R. Haldeman.

"You see?" The Exerciser said. "The battle has barely begun. This deity will use every one of its filthy tricks to beguile us, to divide us, to play on our guilts and fears, but we must be resolute in the face of its onslaught. And now," and he began to remove his outer garments to reveal his gymnast's suit, "I must prepare. First we must start the blood circulating again. She has lain without exercise for many days, and the fat will clog her arteries. Exercise is beneficial."

"Is it?" the evil one lashed out. "You of all people should know how harmful it can be." Then amazingly it switched into the reproachful voice of Parsley, his poor crippled brother. "You did this to me, Romaine. You made me like this," and the demon magically transformed itself into a pitiful hunchback. "See how bent I am, how twisted. When you look like this do you know how hard it is to get dates?

How many chicks want to spend a night in a belltower? You did this to me..."

The voice shook The Exerciser a thousand times more than the blow to the jaw. My brother, he thought, yes, my brother, and a tsunami wave of guilt washed over the shore of his heart, leaving tidepools of regret. But he clenched his fists. "No, no, you are not my brother. You are the demon. And I am going to exercise you."

"No, no, I hate exercise!" the demon rasped, a hint of fear in that ungodly voice, but LeLane grasped the once-beautiful legs now swollen into elephantine pillars and worked them vigorously up and down, reciting as though from a pulpit the text of the Royal Canadian Air Force exercise manual: "Up and down and up and down and up and down..."

Enraged, the thing in Camille spat again, bringing up globs of Roquefort cheese, long-curdled Reddi-Whip, and tapioca pudding that littered the lips and cheeks of its tormentor. Sickened though he was, he wiped the debris away and continued the routine. Now the demon begged piteously, "Stop, LeLane, stop. Let me rest." And the croak changed to Camille's own sweet silvery voice. "Oh, Romaine, you are so handsome, so virile. Why not drop those gym trunks and take out that throbbing manhood of yours, dip it in Mouton Rothschild wine, and put it between my teeth? Yes, let me suck your *coq au vin!* Then swivel around and let me kiss your aspic."

LeLane stood silent, unmovable, undeterred from his purpose. "It is becoming vile again in its food fixation," he said to the two men. He handed Hamilton a book. "Read to her from one of the holy texts."

Hamilton read. "So sayeth Dr. Stillman from the Quick Weight Loss Diet. Ye shall eat naught but lean beef and chicken. Ye shall—" and the demon screamed out its ire, but he kept on—"ingest eggs and cottage cheese and ye shall drink eight glasses of water a day..."

Chow Down glared at the TV tycoon. "So you dare to turn upon me, Hamilton, you Nielsen Rating nincompoop, you Arbitron asshole, you boob-tube bastard! I shall deal with you summarily." The guttural tone vanished, supplanted by the cultured accent of a Bala Cynwyd socialite. "Oh, Foster, my husband, if only you had gone with me that day to the Phillies game, I never would have died. You said a business conference was tying you up. But in truth you were being tied up by your secretary who's into that S-M bag. I knew you were having a thing with her. More than once you came home with whipmarks on your back and lipstick on your shoes."

"Cobina, my wife! It's her!" Hamilton screamed. "I should never have let her go into the upper stands alone. While I was balling she was falling." He wept into his hands, dropping the Stillman text to the floor.

"Don't stop! Defeat the deceit," LeLane said harshly, pulled another holy work from that black bag and handed it to Colin. "Read it quickly."

Colin opened it, rocked slowly back and forth, and read:

> "And Dr. Atkins spake unto the chubby multitudes saying, 'Ye shall eat and enjoy yet not become gross, for ye shall divest yourselves of all carbohydrates.' 'How shall we know we are free of carbohydrates?' they asked, and he replied, 'Ye shall pee onto your ketostix and if they turn purple ye shall be in a state of grace,' and all over the land people did pee on ketostix and pee rained and purple reigned and purple people..."

"Stop that Atkins crap! It cuts into the very heart of my wicked being," the demon commanded.

"No," Colin said.

"Then I'll fix you too, you low-life Cockney scum masquerading as a gentleman," it warned. "Listen, Colin, my unwitting tool, my dupe." And it abandoned the croak again and switched into that dear voice he hadn't heard for so long. "Alfie, my lad, why didn't you bring your poor old Mum over to America? Were you ashamed of me, son? I who suckled you and had enough milk left over for Liverpool, Manchester, and half of Southampton. Hooray, hooray for West Twickham! Kick that ball...."

"Mum, Mum," Colin wept, his tears staining a Dr. Atkins recipe for low-carbohydrate cheesecake. "I should have sent for you. I'm so ashamed..."

LeLane gripped his arm. "Hold on, Colin, it's after you now."

But the demon threw another vocal punch. "I say, Colin, old fig. Why did you make me touch that bloody amulet in the cave? It eventually killed me, you know, and what killed me more is that it left Babs disgustingly wealthy."

Colin staggered against the wall. "My God, that was Sir Roderick Pish-Tepple! Oh, Roderick, forgive me." And the Guilt-O-Meter inside him went higher than the Dow-Jones average before Watergate.

And now the demon piped in an Oriental singsong, "Come, little grass-smoker, see if you can snatch this pebble from my hand. It is wisely written that a man may seek truth in the four comers of the earth and find it, and yet never catch the Number Eight bus to Bergenline Avenue."

"Yentzing, my Sherpa guide," Colin whispered. "It knows everything."

And as though heartened by the weakening of two of its three antagonists, Chow Down roared out a spine-tingling laugh. "Now listen to this voice." And spoke, "Good evening, ladies and gentlemen, and it's a thrill to be here."

"Who is that?" Foster Hamilton said.

"That," said the demon, "was Rich Little's real voice. I just threw it in because no one ever gets a chance to hear it." And then the face contorted again into its hideous gargoyle aspect. "Food, food, food!" And sang:

> *"Gumdrops keep falling on my head,*
> *And I don't care if they are blue or green or red,*
> *Starving's not for me,*
> *Those gumdrops keep falling on my head; they keep falling...*

It thrashed like a harpooned whale, shaking the bedroom, the house, cracking the asphalt in the driveway. "Fooooooooood..."

LeLane said, "If I give you food will you touch your toes ten times?"

"Yes," the demon conceded. "But can I bend my knees?"

"All right, bend your knees—this time," LeLane said.

Cursing and hissing, the demon with a great effort accomplished the ten toe-touches. "Now, LeLannnnnnne... you promised food. And you are a man of your word."

LeLane rummaged in his valise. Took out two stalks of celery. "Here, eat..."

The thing screamed. "No, no, take it away..."

The two pieces of celery in The Exerciser's hand were held in the shape of a cross!

The thing shrank back.

Then LeLane pulled out six carrots which he had previously glued together to form a Star of David. Again the thing trembled. And bellowed, "No, no, you have tricked me, you musclebound motherfucker!"

LeLane took a siphon bottle from the bag and spritzed a violent stream all over the corpulent body. It writhed in sheerest agony, screaming at the top of its lungs, "Oh, it bums, it bums! Seltzer has zero calories. It is the ultimate holy water."

LeLane struck like an adder, commanded it to do ten leg kicks. It fell back exhausted, panting.

"You're beating it!" Colin cried happily.

"Not yet," the physical marvel cautioned. "Now tell me something, evil presence. You referred to Colin as your unwitting tool. That interests me. If you were manipulating him why didn't you possess and swell his body instead of Camille's?"

"I was clever," the demon said in a low voice pregnant with hatred. "If Colin was to tantalize millions and millions of televiewers into overeating, he had to appear trim and handsome. A fat Giggling Gourmet would not have served my purpose. But I punished him in a crueler way by mining his lovely wife, changing her from that hundred-and-five-pound gentle mesomorph into the loathsome endomorph you see before you. It tickled me to glut the slut, to gloat as she would bloat. Now feed me!" It flicked its tongue, vicious as ever.

LeLane knelt before the bed, a shaft of moonlight fell upon the sacred volume in his hand, and he intoned repeatedly in a sepulchral voice, "Bean sprouts... ten-calorie malteds... kohlrabi... fennel..." and each phrase provoked an irate howl from the thing.

Then it happened. A hand snaked out, yanked the book from him, the blanket was kicked away, and the demon spread its legs wide.

"My heaven, it's... it's masturbating with the *Fat Followers Cookbook!*" Colin said.

On pumped the hand, driving the book deeper into the vagina, and the voice said, "Yes, master, I am desecrating this holy work." Satisfied with the shock it had caused, it hurled the soggy cookbook into LeLane's face. "Food! Food!" The voice changed, became a Texas drawl. "Hi y'all, I'm Jimmy Dean. Ain't nothin' so satisfying in the mornin' like muh real good country pork sausages." Then the demon screamed out in its own rasping voice, "Give me pork sausages, LeLane, lots of pork sausages! Slip them between my lips, work them against my tongue. I am the greatest pork-sucker in the universe."

"Camille, my daughter," said Hamilton, who had not uttered a word for two pages. "Is there anything left of you at all or are you completely possessed?"

The eyes looked helplessly out of their fat-swollen casing. The mouth twitched, trying to say something, but could not.

"Look, look on her stomach!" Colin pointed.

Angry red blotches materialized on the mound of bloat that once was her slim waist. As the blotches became clearer, they formed the words HELP ME.

"Thank God, there's something of her left," her father said. "Yes, yes, we'll help you..."

Then there was a mocking laugh and the words seemed to melt and then reform. They now read: FEED ME.

"No, no!" The Exerciser cried. "We shall not fall into that trap again."

The demon slowly began to pull itself up. "Then, Exerciser, we have come to the final moment of confrontation. It is you I was always after, you with your pushups and diets and health foods and clean living and pure mind. You are my mortal enemy."

"Then have it out with me, Chow Down. Free the tiny girl and fight like a man—with a man. Stop beating around the mulberry bush," The Exerciser challenged.

"Mulberries, mulberries," and the popped-out eyes began to swivel madly. "I love mulberries—with milk, sugar, and Wheaties, the breakfast of champions."

"Cease your prattle and fight, oh glutton."

Then the rumble started, deeper, deeper, and deeper, changed to a fierce snarl, then a roar, and the demon's shape began to swell, bigger and bigger, now filling the room, turning at last into its ancient self, the green, potbellied idol, the lips pushed back to reveal the sharp canines. Colin and Foster Hamilton ran into the hallway shrieking in terror, but Romaine LeLane stood his ground, balling up his hands into clubs, his chest swelling, his feet planted like oaktrees...

And the thing roared... and the bed began to shake... and then the bed *rose*... and then with a mighty convulsive heave it lifted the entire 3300 square feet of Levittown Country Clubber ten feet into the air!

But LeLane leaped, dug his steely fingers into a beam, and with every muscle straining he did it...

He pulled the entire house back onto its foundations!

Now the demon's rage was boundless. "You shall die, LeLannnnnnnnne," it screamed. "My very essence shall destroy you!"

And the winds whispered... *Here it is... H-Hour... H for horror... horrendous, horripilating, horrific horror... and, oh boy, that's horror.*

The hulking green idol gave a squeeze from somewhere in its bloated being.

And then it revealed the very nature of what it was.

It was as though giant tubes of toothpaste were being emptied.

From every one of its orifices—mouth, nose, ears, anus, penis—gushed monstrous snakes.

Adipose!

Glistening yellow, buttery snakes of pure fat!

The kind that only surgeons see when they cut into the human body and find it lurking in membranes.

The snakes shot out, entwined themselves around LeLane's chest and began a drive to penetrate his every orifice. He smashed at those hideous thick, yellow worms, driving some of them back, but they were like hydras, branching off into new reptiles with each blow. And in that horrible moment of truth the old lion realized what the demon's game plan was...

To enter and fill him, to bloat him beyond belief, to swarm over and destroy that magnificent physique with legions of strength-sapping, sickening fat.

The force of the assault drove him out of the bedroom window into the garden. And there in the moonlight the titanic war to the death was waged. A smashing right hand from LeLane... a yellow snake exploded into globules of fat... some of the invaders now inside his ears and throat... his mighty fists still pummeling away like windmills... mashing more of them into little blobs... a voice croaking, "Die, LeLannnnnnne, die!"... the strongman answering, "Never... I see who you are now—my ancient enemies, Gluttony, Obesity, Bulemia, Piggishness, Insatiability—but I shall conquer all of you and do it while composing a ballade." As his left hand jabbed at the snakes, his right hand whipped an imaginary white-plumed hat from his head, and he recited with a flourish, sounding amazingly like José Ferrer:

> A gluttonous god named Chow Down,
> Who was thrilled by his worldwide renown,
> Will be sadder and wiser
> When the old Exerciser
> Knocks him clean out of old Levittown!

And the last thing Colin Carew and his father-in-law saw was that heroic tableau, a man, although completely covered by tendrils of unstoppable yellow fat, still battling with indomitable spirit and crying out inexplicably, "Roxanne! Roxanne!"

Then the fat surged on and in, and the beleagured LeLane grew fatter and fatter, swelling like a helium-filled balloon, those craggy features blurred out of shape.

Then an explosion that sent a fireball flashing into the sky. Raining down on the roof of the Country Clubber and the back lawn came fragments of a human being and showers of adipose.

"The stuff got into him and blew him up," Colin sorrowfully said. "The Exerciser is dead."

"But the demon, did it go with him?" Hamilton asked, hoping against hope. "Camille!"

And they rushed for the bedroom.

There she was, wan and exhausted.

But back in her old shapely 105-pound form. Stirring as though awakened from a Rip van Winkle-like sleep.

"Colin?" She looked up. The voice was sweet and silvery once more.

"Camy, darling." He held her closely. "Do you remember anything?"

"No," she said uncertainly. "Oh, wait a minute. I do remember something. It seemed I was in a strange place and a lot of the time it wasn't pleasant at all, but I also remember saying to myself, 'there's no place like home... there's no place like home,' and now I'm home, darling, in my own room, and I'll never go away again from you or daddy or Auntie Em or Toto..."

And the winds whispered. Or rather tried to, but found they could not. They were out of wind.

four

Lt. Christopho was over in ten minutes, eager as usual to give a high-calibre performance. "Uh, pardon me, Mr. Carew, but the neighbors said they heard a scream and an explosion and, uh..."

"Out there," and Colin indicated the garden.

The officer made his preliminary investigation and returned with a chuckle of disbelief. "Geez, some guy out there has been torn limb from limb. I see little pieces of him on the roof, in the flowerbed. Must have taken someone with amazing strength to do that kind of a number on a guy. Is there anybody in this house, who . . and he paused deliberately. "Hey, that's a nice outfit you're wearing. Betcha it cost a pretty penny, huh?"

"About sixty dollars for the sweater, fifty for the slacks."

"Oh yeah? Nice tailoring. And I see your wife has a splendid wardrobe too. She's all better, isn't she?"

"Yes."

"Nice furniture. Nice everything. Well, I guess I'd better fill out this here report."

Colin whispered to him for a few minutes, the lieutenant nodded and scribbled: *Accidental death.* "You know, maybe I oughta leave you a book of these forms. You people seem accident-prone."

He came back in the morning with a U-Haul truck, backed into the driveway, and set about his business.

epilogue

The End of the End

—A week later a FOR SALE sign popped up like a late-blooming crocus on the Carews' front lawn. On the back lawn, where the epic battle to the death had been waged and those yellow blobs of adipose had been scattered, something new was pushing aside the petunias and tulips. *Buttercups.*

—A few days later the Carews emerged from the house, got into a beat-up 1954 Plymouth, and drove away. They carried no bags, no personal effects. In fact, they were stark naked. And since the house was just as naked, thanks to Police Lt. Christopho, there was no need for the Bekins moving men to come and be careful, quick and kind.

—The house was sold in a month to a Prof. Miles Hardaway, but not before he was quizzed extensively by an understandably nervous neighborhood committee spearheaded by the Rosenblatts and Hendersons. Prof. Hardaway explained he was employed by the Army in the field of biological warfare and upon occasion might bring home vials of botulinus for further study. This, they felt, was no stumbling block to their acceptance of him as a good neighbor. Germs, no matter what other characteristics they possessed, were quiet.

—A shaken Father Blatty forsook the cloth and the priest's collar, and is now a necktie salesman in Beverly Hills. Dr. Desmond also gave up the cloth and is seeking the position of the lead singer with the Supremes. So far he has been unsuccessful. He charges racism. With all the cloth his confreres gave up, Rabbi Bindlebinder started a

Seventh Avenue dresshouse and is now president of Lana Frocks, which carries a line of $8.75 to $12.75.

—Lt. Christopho, wearing a natty orange pullover and fawn-colored slacks, made a deposit of $478,990 in the Fidelity National Bank of Philadelphia—somewhat of a coincidence, since that exact amount was withdrawn from the account of Colin Carew. The lieutenant subsequently resigned from the force, purchased a twenty-room mansion in New Hope, Pa., and in a ceremony on his front lawn burned his rumpled raincoat.

—Foster Hamilton, convinced that Colin no longer had any interest whatesoever in anything to do with food and, indeed, would even break into a cold sweat looking at cold cuts, canceled the Giggling Gourmet's TV special. But even though Hamilton himself was revolted by all things culinary, he was still a businessman and knew what the audiences craved. He immediately hired an ex-bordello madam, Xaviera Hollandaise, famous for a sauce that ate you while you were eating it, to host a new show, "The Happy Cooker." The fickle public soon forgot about the handsome Englishman and his wit and recipes.

—The Carews, in order to duck the publicity that had thrown a shadow over their lives, changed their names to Mr. and Mrs. Alfie Pickles. With a small loan from Hamilton, they wound up in Sausalito, Calif., where they opened an art boutique. Colin's charm and wit soon attracted a goodly clientele, and they are now doing nicely. Camille, still pursuing her art career, spends most of her time on the beach, brush in hand, painting the sea. The other day Colin glanced up to see the blue Pacific totally vermillion red from the shoreline to somewhere out past the three-mile limit. "That crazy kid," he said with tenderness. "She actually did paint the sea."

—As for the demon of gluttony, Chow Down, Fresser, Chauser, or however else he is called, did he indeed perish in that electrifying showdown that took the life of The Exerciser?

Somewhere in a Tibetan cave a hoarse voice croaks its sinister threat to the world:

The next time you dig your fork into a lemon meringue pie, beware, I'll be there...

The next time you go ape in an Italian restaurant and cram in a bowl of fettucine Alfredo and butter-saturated garlic bread, and wash it down with a six-pack of Coors Beer, I'll be there...

The next time you sit in front of the TV with Planters Peanuts, the oily kind, and a sack of Granny Goose chips, I'll be there...

And the next time you pile a buffet table with pastrami, corned beef, spiced beef, salami, potato salad, coleslaw, and a ten-pound Pechter's pumpernickel... screw the demon... *we,* the authors, will be there! You know how damn hungry you get, writing a book like this?

about the authors

Sol Weinstein and Howard Albrecht have been collaborating since 1970 on a string of major literary works, including "The Oddfather," "Jonathan Segal Chicken," and "Oh Henry!" They have also written for some of the top TV shows and performers: Sammy Davis Jr., Alan King, Milton Berle, Jonathan Winters, Dinah Shore, etc. Weinstein, who earlier authored the Israel Bond, Secret Agent Oy Oy Seven spy thrillers and "Everything You Never Wanted to Know About Sex," hails from Trenton, New Jersey, and Levittown, Pennsylvania, and drew from the latter locale an incident of caloric possession upon which "The Exerciser" is based. He currently lives in California. His main hobby is having anxiety attacks. Albrecht, a former New York City executive for a chain of sportswear stores, also resides in California where he spends his leisure hours enjoying sexual fantasies far beyond his physical capabilities. Both authors have been on continuous diets since the prenatal period.

Note: this is from the original edition. Mr. Albrecht still lives in California. Mr. Weinstein, alas, does not still live anywhere.

If you enjoyed this book...

...or if you enjoy getting books that you don't enjoy, then look for the full run of Sol Weinstein's Israel Bond Oy-Oy-7 books wherever you got this book. (Unless you found it on a bus or something, because, really, what are the odds of repeating that sort of stroke of amazingly good luck?)

Also available for the Kindle, the Nook, the iPad, and other electronic devices.

Oy-Oy-7.com

www.ingramcontent.com/pod-product-compliance
Lightning Source LLC
LaVergne TN
LVHW011203080426
835508LV00007B/566